NO PROPS

Great Games with No Equipment

by Mark Collard

Illustrations by Michelle Dybing

ISBN-13: 978-0-934387-05-7

Book design and production by:
SYP Design & Production, Inc.
www.sypdesign.com

Acknowledgments

Thank you so much to the following people. I tell you in person how much I value you. This is to express my gratitude publicly.

- Karl Rohnke, whose inspiration and efforts to help create an innovative and fun learning model called Project Adventure sparked my initial foray into the adventure programming world. Today, his friendship and encouragement continue to fuel my desire to keep writing.

- The Project Adventure team worldwide, especially in Australia, for providing much of the fodder for this volume of two-finger typed devotion, and the opportunity to play. In particular, I take my hat off to Don MacDowall, Karen Rawady, Steve Whitmore and Bill Thompson in Australia and Dick Prouty, Jane Panicucci, Mary Henton, Adam Clark, Rufus Collinson, Lisa Hunt, Mark Murray, David Baldridge, Amy Kohut, and Rich Klajnscek who are scattered throughout the rest of the Project Adventure world.

- My family, who continue to wait patiently for me to get a "real" job.

- Michelle Dybing for providing the wonderful illustrations that really capture the essence of the activities.

- To all the wonderful people who, over the years, have accepted my invitation to play. You have inspired many of the fun activities and their variations found within these pages.

Thank you so much. It's been real – real fun!

Structure of the Book

In the finest traditions of my programmatic kitchen, here is a sneak preview of the four-course menu I have prepared for you.

Introduction

Starters (Appetizers)

- **We should take fun more seriously** – Fun and play form the backbone of this publication. Indulge me as I muse for a moment and acknowledge the extraordinary value that a generous serving of fun can bring to a program…by bringing out the best in folks.
- **Programming Philosophies** – The glue that binds all of the most successful programs together. Embrace whatever activity you can think of within the framework of these simple philosophies, and I expect that you will find it will take on a whole new dimension, and, very likely, achieve greater success.
- **Things I've learned along the way** – Ruminations of some of the most compelling pearls of programming wisdom that I can offer from my more than twenty years of playful experience. They are the subtleties of my facilitation that I believe have made a significant difference to the way I invite groups to play, trust and learn.
- **Group-splitting exercises** – Have you ever gotten tired of asking people to "find a partner," and wished that there was another way? Then, this section is for you.

Main Meal

The activities have been broadly categorised according to their most common use.

- **Ice-breakers** – to set the tone, invite people to interact and laugh; all of which build the foundations of a successful program
- **Warm-ups** – to energise people, and perhaps invite them to stretch a little – physically and emotionally
- **Tag Games** – especially for those who have plenty of energy to spare, or simply enjoy the wild abandon of a good chase
- **Trust Exercises** – activities which are primarily focused on developing trust and strengthening relationships, or that simply embrace the finer moments of our being human
- **Group problem-solving activities** – ideal for developing communication, leadership and co-operation skills. Activities that challenge a group to pool their collective resources, solve the problem and then reflect back on what they have achieved / learned.

In all cases, every activity that is shared between these covers is enhanced with at least one variation, and often many more. So, really, you're picking up a vast treasure chest of programming ideas, perfect for any group, especially if you have no props.

Sweets (Desserts)

Beyond the pure, unadulterated pleasure of playing these games, you may discover some further intrinsic value in them – it's just that your group doesn't need to know about it! You can reward your group by leaving the "dessert"

until the end, or if you're like me, you'll be tempted to punctuate your programmatic menu with a little "sweetness" throughout. No matter – they are all about having fun.

Tea & Coffee

That part of the book where you can sit back and relax, and rub your tummy as you ponder the value of a good meal. A brief section in which I've included some references for you to find further resources relevant to the adventure programming field, just in case you've still got room for more.

Contents

Introduction

An invitation to play

When I was growing up, my adrenaline would literally burst out of my skin when I heard someone call to me, "Wanna come out and play?" These moments were golden. Like a duck to water, I would drop everything and eagerly take up the invitation. Well, I stand before you now and invite you to do just that – come out and play.

Of course, it is not necessary, nor recommended, to stand idly by at the precipice of play, waiting to be invited. Opportunities for play can occur at all times and, in my experience, mostly when you least expect them.

Consider the following moments, and try to catch yourself thinking about the last time one or more of them happened to you:

- You have five minutes to fill before the start of the next session, class, whatever.

- Your group has that "what are we going to doooo?" look on their faces.

- The equipment you so meticulously stored last night is now missing, or worse, it just broke.

- The clip-board you are holding is worth slightly more than your program's annual budget.

- Your out-of-doors program has just been washed out.

- You simply want to have an outrageously fun time.

This book is dedicated to these very moments. There can be no more valuable resource than a large repertoire of activities that can be pulled out of your hat on cue, anytime, anywhere. That's what this book is all about. It is full of dozens of sure-fire, high-energy, interactive, leave-them-asking-for-more activities – all of which require no equipment.

My original intentions were to simply share a list of the best "no-props" activities that I had led and / or experienced. But, much like the preparation of a delicious meal, no matter how good the ingredients are, the success of the meal will rely heavily on a good recipe. Accordingly, a series of "fun" activities played one after the other does not necessarily create a fun and successful experience for everyone. The key is the approach that is taken in the design and delivery of the activities.

About Project Adventure

It is more than just the name of an organisation. Project Adventure is a way of doing, an approach to working with people that has helped millions to exceed their perceived boundaries, work with others to solve problems and experience success.

Project Adventure, an international, non-profit organisation, began in 1971 as an innovative tenth-grade physical education program based in part on the principles of Outward Bound. Understanding that adventure was more about doing and less about where and what one does, PA's founders developed a program that could be done indoors or on a playing field, accessed by "students" of all abilities and adaptable to many different time frames.

The program consisted of non-traditional games, warm-ups, trust exercises, group problem-solving activities – many similar to those found in this book – and the use of low and high Challenge Course elements. Students learned to work cooperatively, challenge themselves in a supportive environment, improve self-esteem and learn creative approaches to problem-solving. Yet, all of this occurred without the need to trek in the wilderness, or other such "high adventure."

Our goal is simple – "to bring the adventure home." Today, with more than 30 years of experience and offices throughout the United States, Australia, New Zealand, Japan and Singapore, Project Adventure has introduced and helped adapt adventure into literally thousands of academic, corporate, therapeutic and community-based programs.

We maintain a strong belief that a learning environment that utilises adventure and cooperative learning techniques in a supportive environment is an optimal educative experience. Hence, this approach is important for all "students," no matter where the "classroom" is found. Fun is also a major element because, in our experience, people learn more effectively if they enjoy what they are doing. Fun helps to engage people, thereby providing opportunities for growth.

Sharing this way of doing with others is what we do. We continue to create new activities and props; author new and leading-edge publications for the field; offer trainings that help to develop the skills needed to implement this innovative program approach safely and effectively; and provide consultation services to help you develop, apply and maintain a quality program.

No Props Glossary

It's strange how we can use a common language (English), and yet find that we can't understand each other at times. Such is the curiosity of slang, or put lexicographically, the use of very informal words, phrases or meanings not regarded as standard, or used by a specific group of people.

The following is a list of words and phrases that are well understood by blokes and sheilas in Orstraya (er, men and women who call Australia home), but are described here for the reference of our American friends.

Baulk
Refuse to go on, hesitate, thwart and hinder, as in *I baulked at the idea.* Or just another word that we have decided to retain the "u" – as in favourite, colour, etc.

Chasey
Hip name for a tag game, as in *Let's play a game of 'kiss-chasey.'*

Come a cropper
To fall heavily or fail badly, as in *Did you see Jim come a cropper off his horse?*

Come in spinner
Colloquial term cried out by a gambler just as they are throwing the dice, or spinning the roulette wheel, as in *"Ohhhhh, I'm feeling lucky tonight… come in Spinner."*

Fair-dinkum
True, genuine, reliable, as in *I wouldn't lie to you mate, fair dinkum!*

In situ
In its original place, as in *The evidence was photographed in situ before it was removed.*

Keen
Enthusiastic, eager and sharp, as in *She was keen to get inside out of the cold.*

Lepidoptery
The study of butterflies and moths, as in *My father is a lepidopterist.*

Lolly
A sweet, piece of confectionery, as in *Here's five cents to buy a bag of mixed-lollies.*

Mondo
Large number, lots or way too much to quantify, as in *I think we will need mondo chairs to seat everyone.*

Monkey Grip
When two people join hands, where the fingers of each person curl inside the palm of their partner, and the thumbs sit on top, as in *Grab my hand in a monkey grip and hold tight.*

Ocker
Rough, boorish and aggressively Aussie male, characterised by a discernable, but somewhat loveable, vulgarity, as in *He has such an ocker attitude towards women.*

Office dogs body
Person who does all the drudge, mundane, boring tasks, as in *I worked for two years at XYZ as the general office dogs body.*

Petal

Highfalutin, pompous term used by the eccentric, rich and famous to refer to another person, as in *Dear Petal, I couldn't possibly think of anything worse than putting my hands in dishwater...*

Stacks on the Mill

Where several people are piled up chaotically, one on top of the other, often with some wretched person on the bottom, as in *Hey, let's get Mick! – stacks on the mill...*

Ta

Thank you, I appreciate that, as in *You should always say "ta" when you are given something.*

Titters

Laugh in a furtive or restrained way, girlish giggle, as in *The joke left the girls in titters.*

Tiggy

Another hip way to refer to a tag game, see chasey.

Walking on spot

The motion of leg and foot movements to give the impression that a person is walking, but in fact he / she is not moving off an imaginary spot, as in *A mime artist is very good at walking on spot.*

Works a treat

Wonderful outcome, what is desired, as in *A lolly at the end of the day works a treat.*

STARTERS (APPETIZERS)

WE SHOULD TAKE FUN MORE SERIOUSLY!

To invite people to play, perhaps encounter an "adventure" of sorts, an atmosphere of safety and support needs to exist. To this end, we should take fun more seriously.

Don't laugh – this is serious. Sounds like a misnomer of terms doesn't it? But, it's true; we should take fun – or play – more seriously.

Have you ever noticed that adults don't play anymore? I mean really play, in the true sense of the word. Sure, we play organised sport, play the odd board game or put on a play, but none of these really capture the true essence of play. There is seldom any freedom, or true self-expression in the adult forms of play. Sadly, when we think we're "at play," we too often feel compelled to set a few rules, throw in some high level skills, and smother it with goals. There's nothing necessarily wrong with this, but I believe there's more to play than meets than eye, and we should do more of it. I guess that's what this book, and Project Adventure in particular, aims to encourage.

To play is to participate without a care for the why, who or what. Watch a group of young children left alone in a park, and observe the games they play. Activity just emerges, rules are kept to a minimum, everyone is involved, laughter is plentiful, and at the end of the day, they positively glow with that conspicuous "that-was-great-I-feel-great" air. And I betcha that if you were to ask any of these children at the end what they were doing, they would very likely say "ummm, nothing much." We truly play when we engage with others simply for the fun, laughter and pure joy our interaction can draw from a situation, with whomever, and for whatever reason you choose to think of, or not. There are no winners as such, just lots of doing, and a celebration of life. A freedom to be.

Play Trust Learn

One of my favourite Project Adventure t-shirts has the words "Play Trust Learn" emblazoned on the back. I've lost count of the number of people who have come up to me (in the midst of a program I am delivering, or a supermarket aisle!) and commented "Hey, I like what that says." Well, so do I – in fact, I believe in it.

There's an old saying that suggests that you can learn more about someone from an hour of play, than from a year of conversation. People discover things about themselves, and about others that will surprise them. They will laugh, they will share, and before you know it, they are dismantling barriers to relationships that have stood the test of time. I think of the most serious, intrinsic corporate team-development programs I have led which, I believe, gained more value from the silly, little games that we played, than the predictable sit-down-and-talk-about-teamwork sessions.

We all know that trust and communication are the keys to a healthy relationship – well, that's what play and having fun is all about. It works so well because you don't see it coming. You simply play, you share, you interact and you trust. And, because it's fun, it's infectious and hard to resist. There is something magnetic about play that when properly framed, brings out the best in folks. And, better still, when it's conducted in an atmosphere that is fun and supportive, people learn stuff too.

PROGRAMMING PHILOSOPHIES: A WAY OF DOING

(see *TEA & COFFEE section for expanded discussion of these philosophies*)

A series of "fun" activities played one after the other, however, does not instinctively create a fun and successful experience for everyone. In my experience, the key to success is the approach that is taken in the design and delivery of all the activities – that is, the way you do things. The whole package – not just the right activities, but the right approach, and the right situation – will directly impact on how much fun it creates for everyone, including you.

Sequencing

Using the right activity at the right time.

Challenge by Choice

Giving people a choice to determine their own level of participation.

Note: Participants will have varying levels of comfort with being in close physical proximity to other people as they engage in the activities. Be certain that Challenge by Choice is in full operation and that people have options about how they use their bodies.

FUNN

A whimsical acronym for Functional Understanding Not Necessary, suggesting that fun for its own sake is okay.

The Full Value Contract

A powerful cultural framework that can help groups to guide their work, manage their behaviours and play together more safely and effectively.

Experiential Learning Cycle

A tool that can help participants elicit more from an experience than just having fun, i.e., when you want to crank up the intrinsic side of fun.

This is just a glimpse of Project Adventure's simple, yet powerful approach to programming. For an expanded discussion, **see page 213.**

THINGS I'VE LEARNED ALONG THE WAY

Many years ago, I started to record a list of all the activities I had been exposed to – mostly as a participant – during my Project Adventure experiences. Reflecting my fastidious inclinations, I grouped like activities together, so that as the list grew longer and longer, I would find it easier to access them when I needed a good idea. Ice-breakers, de-inhibitizers, warm-ups, initiatives, trust exercises, games – I recorded the lot.

Twenty years later, the list has grown into what I refer to now as my "Book of Tricks," or, when feeling particularly enamoured, my "bible." There are simply hundreds of great activity ideas contained between its seriously dog-eared covers. Yet, as much as it represents a chronicle of what I have played over the years – and continue to draw benefit from – it would fail to inform even the most learned of my colleagues the slightest glimpse of what I have discovered along the way. And, most importantly, what I believe to be more significant than the games themselves.

As I flip through its pages, I know for a fact that my briefing, presentation and understanding of many of the earliest recorded activities has changed significantly – for the better – since I first played them. It's true, I have added many new and wonderful variations to my list of games, but this is not the difference I speak of. Rather, I refer to the philosophies and general comprehension of how play can develop positive relationships that now envelop my facilitation style and overall program delivery approach.

As a senior international trainer for Project Adventure, I often muse about these differences for the benefit of training participants. Now, I think it's time to write them down.

Frame, frame, frame

In other words, prepare, prepare, prepare. Appropriately framing an activity – that is, "setting the scene," or providing a context in which the activity will take place – is one of the most valuable tools I employ to help groups achieve their goals, i.e., be successful. Otherwise, your group may be emotionally under-prepared for what is about to happen.

People have a natural proclivity to want to know why they are doing what they are doing. Framing goes a long way toward answering these questions, as well as reducing anxiety, providing clarity, and generally coaxing people forward into your program.

Everything you do programmatically provides the context in which the next activity is framed. For example:

(i) Your language – it's not just what you say, but how you say it – check out the next paragraph for a more thorough discussion.

(ii) Lead-up activities – like building blocks, every activity should aim to complement the next, rather than subvert it. To illustrate, leading into a serious discussion with a very energetic, bounce-off-the-wall type of activity is unlikely to result in a settled, composed or focused group of people.

(iii) Your general approach to facilitation – if you operate under the premise of Challenge by Choice, but your overall demeanour says there is no choice, you are likely to turn people off.

Ask yourself, "Have I done everything to prepare my group – emotionally and physically – for this experience?" "Do they know what they are getting into, and why?" If not, think about what lead-up activities you could use to prepare the way, or perhaps what introduction / briefing might be necessary to soothe the group into the activity.

It's all in how you say it

As a participant, which would you prefer to hear?

> "….and if you're too slow, or get the wrong answer, you are "out" and you have to come into the centre of the circle….."

> Or, "…and if the time expires, or you make a gaffe, you are invited to take your turn in the centre of the circle and have some fun….."

Perhaps each statement is saying the same thing, but for many people, they will hear a big difference. The first implies that I have no choice ("you have to"), so I might feel under pressure because I don't want to be "slow" or "wrong." This may manifest itself as, "I don't want to make a mistake, so perhaps I won't play." While the second statement is all about options (you may decline the invitation), and fun is introduced as an integral part of the consequence of "going out."

As program providers, our language is one of our most potent tools. It can work for us or against us, and I don't just mean the use of "politically correct" terms. Beware that everything you say, from the moment you introduce yourself to the moment that you wave good-bye will fan the flames of invitation and play, or snuff them out.

Ask yourself, "Have I introduced this activity in the most appealing, inclusive, way?" Provide choices to people so that they can find a level of participation that is comfortable for them.

Inject lots of humour

This is such a critical element of delivery, and the key to opening up your group. Observe the crazy, menial little things people do, and serve it back to them in a manner that says, "Have you ever noticed this?" Of course, they have, they just don't want to admit it.

For example, the insistence some people have for tagging one another after the game has stopped, or the understated crawling on knees when a simple pivot in place was called for. Or, at a more serious level, the subtle glance over the shoulder to check that your spotters really are there behind you to catch your fall, even though the command "Ready, fall away!" was given. What about the way we (notice, I'm using the royal "we" here, so as to not draw attention to myself) avert our eyes and attention away from someone whose name we have once known, but now that they are coming our way, cannot for all the rice in China remember it? I could go on and on….

Suffice it to say, people love this stuff – it was the essence of the TV show *Seinfeld*. Our programs are made up of so much normalness, perhaps nothingness, it can be hilarious to sit back and look at it for what it really is at times. Of course, how you deliver these moments is key – what could appear to some as a diamond in the rough, may just be a rock to others. Focus your humour so that you encourage your group to laugh with rather than at others.

Oh, and inject tons of FUNN too – it will act as a magnet for many more moments of people simply being human!

Let the group create its own energy or, If you build it, they don't always come!

Having just encouraged you to inject lots of humour, I have to admit, that some groups just don't get it. You can lay out the most fun-filled, most inviting program ever, and yet, they still won't come to the party. In the early days, a typical reaction from yours truly to this scenario was to work even harder, and generate the energy myself that I was looking to come from the group. After "hitting the wall" on several occasions, I finally got it.

Give yourself and your group permission to discover its own energy. It will be different for every group, and provided you have created a caring and supportive environment within which to play, wherever the group is at, is where the group is supposed to be. End of story. Sure, pepper your program with a little more levity, but do not generate the energy for the group solely on your own efforts. You will burn yourself out way too quickly, and importantly, you will rob (read, disempower) your group of the opportunity to be the cause of its own outcomes.

How not to pick a partner

Have you ever noticed how the seemingly innocuous words "Okay, everybody pick a partner...." can strike terror into the hearts of many participants? In my experience, it is one of the most frightening things you can ask a group to do. Questions such as "Should I pick someone, or wait to be picked?", "What if I pick somebody, and they don't want to play with me?", "Does she really want to play with me, or is she just being nice", or "If I pick him, will he think I'm coming on to him?" will be roused among many others.

Sadly, the instruction to "pick a partner" is too-oft interpreted as "find someone you are attracted to." This thought is as embarrassing as it is open to the anxiety-laden prospect of people feeling left out. There are just too many other ways to ask people to get into smaller groups, including pairs, to risk these outcomes.

Now, I'm not suggesting that you should never use the words "Pick a partner" again. Certainly, as a program develops and your group becomes more comfortable with one another, the panic-inducing reaction to simply "picking a partner" will diminish. But, with most groups, especially if they have just met each other, you are well advised to avoid the typical "pick a partner" suggestion.

Check out the Group-Splitting Excercises on page 20 for some amusing, often random methods to help in the selection of partners or small groups.

Always ask for a volunteer

There is always, no matter how long you wait, someone willing to step into the ring of fire, and help you do whatever you need. Perhaps you need help to demonstrate the next move, or need someone to break the ice and start the activity, whatever – it never fails, there is always someone willing to step forward.

But why bother, when you can often save time and potential embarrassment by doing it yourself, or asking a colleague to step in? The value is hidden in the invitation.

It can be as simple as observing the initial humour of no one stepping forward, or everyone but one poor soul stepping back. However, beyond the humour, there is extraordinary value in using a volunteer from your group. Having one or more of your group step forward says "I am willing to… take a risk, have fun, give it a go, look silly," etc, etc. These are huge transformative messages that are broadcast loud and clear – yet subtly – to the rest of the group. It will frequently open up further opportunities for more of this, from more of your group.

Asking for volunteers is part of the fun, it's suspenseful ("what's he/she gonna do?"), and it's a true adventure, especially if you don't telegraph what they are going to be doing. Besides, I get to be up-front all the time. I want to share the limelight from time to time.

Have more up your sleeve than you need

You can never have too many activities lined up in your head, or too much equipment at the ready. This could just be another way of saying, "Be prepared," but it's more than that. It's about options.

Stuff happens – the bus arrives late, it starts to rain, the room is smaller than you anticipated, a member of your group is nursing an injury or disability, etc, etc – all of these events call for immediate attention. Sometimes, it may be just as simple as getting to the end of your activity list, and realising

too late that the program ran for much less time than you had imagined.

I can't tell you the number of times I have been "saved" from that menacing what-are-we-going-to-do-now? look by resorting to Plan B, C or D, and making it look like I had it all planned from the start. It's always better to say "….Gee, I didn't get to do half of what I wanted, or planned, etc " than "…arghhhh, I need to think of something quick…". It makes you look good too!

Stop an activity before it wanes

Leave them wanting for more. Stopping an activity just as it reaches its peak, and perhaps a tad further will give you many useful programmatic starting points. Moving on at this juncture keeps the energy of the group up, and their spirits high. It's easier to slide into the next activity if you have their attention, even if they are complaining that you stopped too soon. Better this than having no complaints because everyone left the scene on account of eventual boredom!

You can always go back to the activity if it really is that good (and it fits your program goals), but it's often better to move onto something new while you have them in the palm of your hand.

And remember, quoting the evangelical words of Karl Rohnke, if "at the end of the day you have waned more often than you waxed, get a new job."

Try new things all the time

It's easy to fall into the pattern of repeating the same old same old, for no other reason than that it works. And that is good, but there's a lot to be said for trying out some new stuff too. Indeed, seek out new stuff. Experiment with some new activities, or change the prop or the scenario, even the reason for doing it – just because you can.

I'll even trot out an old activity I didn't really like much and haven't used in years, just to see if my suspicions hold true. Sometimes they do, but not always – and that's the key. You'll never grow in terms of your confidence, your repertoire and your experience, unless you give "new" a go.

Your comfort zones will stretch too, which is what many of our programs are about, right? Which brings me to my next pearl of programmatic wisdom…..

Walk your talk

Example is a powerful cause in people's life. If your group sees you do the very thing you are asking them to do, they are more likely to take it on. This is one of the primary reasons I love my work, because I get to play and join in on the fun, rather than stand back all the time.

But more than just participating, walking your talk embraces everything about your program and who you are to your group – from the language you use and encourage, to the choices you make and respect – it all matters. If you can mix it with your group (when it is appropriate) and demonstrate that you are prepared to take risks (for example, in the challenges you set, and the types of activities you use), your example will inspire your group to have fun and take risks too.

Naturally, there are times when you need to step back, and let your group play and learn on their own. However,

accept that some groups like nothing more than to see their teacher, leader, coach, whoever, do the activity with them.

One further nudge – I surmise that about 95% of the activities I know and deliver I have learned through actually doing them. Be it as a participant of someone else's program, or an activity that I've just picked up from somewhere (i.e., a book or a peer), pretty much all of the activities I do, I have done as a participant. I also strongly believe that this experience – knowing what it's like to be a participant in the activity (as distinquished from being the leader) – will make you a much better facilitator of the activity. Actual get-your-hands-dirty participation will give you direct knowledge of what it's like to be a participant in the activity – which no book or learned colleague's stories about a new, you-beaut activity could ever substitute. It will also keep you fresh, you know, in a way that reminds you of what it's like to be a participant again.

And if all of this has failed to convince you to walk your talk, just do it for the fun.

Play on

Ever been left out of a group? Ever felt that everyone else was having fun, but you weren't? You're not on your own – I've been there, and done that, especially when I was younger. So I make it a point not to introduce too many activities that eliminate people, especially early in a program.

Games that eliminate folks can be great fun; I still use many of them. But when used at the wrong time, or in the initial stages of a group's development, it risks alienating certain people, not to mention losing a lot of useful energy. Also, it is not unusual to watch the same people get eliminated over and over again. Beware of the message this may send to the group – and the individual – if this does not occur within a safe and supportive atmosphere.

Clearly, the more people you have involved, the more energy and good times you can develop – which is my next point.

Keep people bunched together

The wall-flower syndrome – you know, those folks who like to stand with their backs to the wall – is a real killer of energy and enthusiasm, especially in the beginning stages of your program (when it seems everyone is reading the same script). Always invite people to come closer to you, get them to bunch up a little. Circles work fine, but when you don't need a circle, collapse them in, and invite them to move closer to you. You and they will bristle with energy, which is a wonderful way to kick-off.

My style is very much "Hey, come over here. I've got a secret to tell". People move in. They lean closer.

Their attention is piqued. I love that. They are now primed, and ready to rock-n-roll. Yet, at the same time, the group has started to unconsciously break down some barriers, not to mention, trust and share. This is all good.

Try speaking a little softer. That often works a treat. Your group will have to bunch up together simply to hear you. And all those folks who can't hear you because they are too busy talking, will suddenly gasp when they realise the group has gone quiet! I love the humour of that moment too.

Oh, there is just one caveat – never ask a very large group of over-enthusiastic children standing in a circle, to take a few steps into the centre towards you – before you know it, you will be under the biggest pile of "stacks on the mill" you've ever had the back-breaking pleasure to be a part of.

Seek feedback all the time

Finally, if you are keen to improve your program skills, one of the best things you can do for yourself is to seek feedback. And the best time to do this, is when you don't want to hear the answers. Yes, you read that correctly; it's often the things that we don't want to hear that moves us forward.

Seek feedback from your peers and colleagues in particular. Sure, you can ask your participants and program clients for feedback, but their opinion will rarely go beyond the standard "Oh, that was really good", or "That sucked!" remarks. Discussing your progress with someone who knows what it takes to be a good program provider will inspire greater insight and a more meaningful response. Comments such as "Your assessment of the group's skills at X point was brilliant", or "Try to ask simple questions at the beginning of your debrief" are good examples of specific, constructive feedback.

It's not always possible, but try to work alongside other colleagues as often as your program and / or budget will allow. Sharing the lead with one or more people can be a lot of fun, and will provide you with a number of perspectives from which to receive pointers, advice and praise.

GROUP-SPLITTING EXCERCISES

There are literally oodles of activities out there that will keep your whole group active doing the same thing at the same time. As such, once your group has assembled, they are ready to go. But, there are just as many large group activities that work more effectively if you, first, split your aggregation into smaller groupings. Indeed, this strategy can be a very useful way to "warm" your group up, and in particular build their skills gradually working from smaller to larger units.

So, how do you divide your group?

Let's say you've got fifty people, and need five groups – that'll make ten people per group, right? Yes, but how do you decide which ten goes into which group? The composition of each group, and the manner in which the members are chosen can make a big difference to the outcome of an activity – not to mention how each member may feel about their belongingness. Take, for example, two traditional group-splitting methods that I can remember from way-back in high school (and twenty-five years on, I know they still get used):

(a) The teacher / leader picks two (or more) "captains" and the captains pick their own teams. Just fine if you're friends with one of the newly appointed. But, an unmitigated disaster if you are – like me – one of the smallest, less-coordinated kids on the block. The result – an argument mounted by each team at the end of the choosing as to why the other team should have to take me.

Like I said, not a good self-esteem building exercise.

(b) Then there's the old count-off method – 1, 2, 3, 4, 1, 2, 3, 4, and so on. Have you ever noticed how people will often move their place in the line just so that they will get a number they want, i.e., that which matches their friends'? Or worse, short of branding a number on people's foreheads, how do you police who is in whose group anyway?

Sure, these methods can work. But, rarely do they produce balanced teams (in terms of players, skills levels or both), and are about as much fun as they are self-esteem building exercises – not! So – da da – here is a collection of some of my favourite group-splitting methods, each of them inspired by a number of fun variations.

Consider the size of your group, the number of smaller groups you want to establish, and how much time you would like to devote to the splitting process. This third factor is helpful because many of the following ideas (all with tons of variations) are fun to play just for their own delectation. All you need is some open space to spread folks out, and as many of them as you can muster. Enjoy!

In addition to the exercises listed below, you may also want to check out these activities.

Categories – **see page 31**
Psychic Handshake – **see page 36**
Clumps – **see page 32**
Look Up – Look Down – **see page 127**

SNAPPY PARTNERS

Some of the quickest, easiest ways to find a partner, or a group

WHAT TO DO

As described in an earlier section, there is nothing worse than being asked to "find a partner" as you stare into a sea of unknown and quite frightening new faces. It's much easier if you can direct the traffic somewhat, and here are a few ideas which will diminish a lot of that initial anxiety.

Ask your group to:

- Find another person with a similar colour top, or socks, or zodiac, length of hair as you, or who hops on the same foot as you, has the same number of letters in their name, etc.
- Form a circle facing inwards, and on your command, "look down" at the ground, and then on your command, ask everyone to "look up" to the eye level of other group members. If two people happen to look at each other (i.e., by chance), they depart the scene as newly-formed partners, the circle contracts, and the pairing continues. This is a similar set-up to Look Up Look Down on page 127.
- Stand next to a friend / someone they know. Ask one of the pair to kneel down, and the other to remain standing. Then, ask all those who are standing to move to one side, and voila, you have two even teams – and you have likely separated friends / cliques.
- Same as above, but ask one partner to put their hands on their head, while the other puts their hands on their (own) bottom.
- Everyone extends a certain number of fingers on one (or two) hands behind their back. Once ready, ask everyone to reveal their variously extended digits in front of them so that others can see them – the task is to find another person with the same number of exposed fingers.
- Form one straight line – according to a random fit, or by way of a particular criteria such as height, date of birth, the last two digits of their home telephone number, etc – and then fold the resulting line in the middle so that it collapses back on itself. Each person ends up facing another person to become partners.
- Form a pair (by using one of the above methods), and then join up with another pair to form a group of four, and then this aggregation joins with a new group of four to obtain a group of eight, etc.
- Each person sings out loud the sound of the first vowel of their name, and seeks an equally harmonic partner, or partners as the case requires.
- Ask each person in your group to think of three (or whatever number of groups you need) animals. In one huge cacophonic symphony, ask each person to rapidly and loudly make the sound of all three (or whatever number) of animals for approx ten seconds. Then, ask everyone to shut their eyes, imagine that all but one of the animals have run away, and when they next open their eyes, they are to make only the noise of the animal they have imagined is left remaining (i.e., it is presumed that not everyone will imagine the same animal). Similar creature sounds are the cue for partnership.

PICK A NUMBER OUT OF A HAT

Some fun, new possibilities for a "golden oldie"

WHAT TO DO

You will need to prepare a little in advance for this group-splitting technique. Find a large receptacle – such as an empty tin can, or a hat – and collect (or cut) as many small pieces of paper as you have people in your group.

Next, you need to decide on a theme that all the pieces of paper will have in common, and then a list of unique identities within that theme. For example, let's say you are looking to form ten groups out of 90 people. You could choose animals as your theme (or any one of the ideas listed below), then list ten different types of animals such as lions, bears, eagles, etc. Write the name of each animal on nine pieces of paper (i.e., each group will have nine players in it). Perhaps fold the pieces of paper up a little (to prevent sneaky hand-picked glances), stuff them all in a big tin can, and you're ready to go.

As you distribute the pieces of paper, ask your group not to show them to other people, nor tell them what is written on it. It's a secret! Then, once all of the pieces have been handed out, explain what it is they have to do. Basically, the goal is for everyone to find other looks-or-sounds-like-me people to form a group.

Here are a few ideas that will help to inspire some fun group-sorting banter.

Numbers

- Announce your number to the world, or use out-stretched fingers, or even claps to indicate your number.

- Shake your hand with another person (as you greet them) according to your number (see Psychic Handshake on page 36)

Animals

- Make the sound of the animal (be sure to use animals that have audible sounds/calls).
- Mime / act the look of the animal.

Word Associations

- Announce your "word" or simply show your piece of paper, as you mingle about the group, and try to find other people with:

  (i) The same "word" or
  (ii) A word that is typically associated with your word, e.g., peanut + butter, coca + cola or
  (iii) An object that fits within a particular category, e.g., some folks may be holding "Cadillac," "Holden," and "Ford" (make of car), while others in the group hold "rose," "tulip," or "daffodil" (type of flower).

Action Oriented

- Demonstrate the action written on the piece of paper, i.e., everyone who performs same action are in the same grouping. For example:

  Scratch my back
  Pinch me
  Pull my ear
  Clap your hands

Tickle me
Hold my hand
Rub my tummy
Whistle a tune

Hum Dinger

- Hum the tune of a popular song / nursery rhyme, etc.
- Whistle the tune of a popular song / nursery rhyme, etc.

Sweet thing

- Rather than paper, distribute lollies. Ask people to eat the lolly – such as a jellybean – and divide up according to the colour of their tongue.

What if you don't know how many people are coming? This is especially true for large conference type gatherings, or public events.

Theory would suggest that if the pieces of paper are sufficiently mixed, each team will have roughly the same number of members, regardless of how many people attend. But, if your activity relies on each team having a specific number of people, I recommend strategically releasing more pieces of paper as more people arrive. For example, let's say you need teams of ten people, and you anticipate that 120 people could arrive at the most. Make up 12 categories of ten "things" and distribute sufficient pieces to fill, say, six teams in the beginning. Then, as more people arrive, add a new "team" of ten pieces to the tin. If you do this next step twice, you will end up with eight teams of approx ten people, rather than 12 teams of seven people or so (if you had distributed all of the 12 teams at the start).

PUZZLE PIECES

*A really creative way to help people mix with one another,
and find their grouping*

WHAT TO DO

You'll need to either purchase a set of pre-fabricated blank cardboard puzzle sets, or simply make up a set of puzzles for yourself from coloured sheets of cardboard. In each case, you will want one complete puzzle set for every group you wish to form, and ideally the same number of puzzle pieces as you have members in a group.

Once the puzzles have been selected / created, place all of the pieces into a big bag, mix them up, and when your group has assembled, ask each person to select one piece for themselves. Now, instruct each person to find everyone else who holds a piece of the same puzzle, with a view to re-building the puzzle.

Try to make each of the puzzles very unique, and quite distinct in appearance to all the others, i.e., no two pieces should look alike, nor should one piece fit into the frame of another puzzle. One easy way to achieve this is to "paint" the back of each puzzle with a unique colour, or to use a "picture."

A word of caution – do not make the puzzle too difficult to assemble. Timing will vary, but anything more than five to ten minutes is too long, and will start to diminish the time you had prepared for the "main event" – the reason for wanting small groups in the first place.

A suggestion – the puzzle, once it is put back together, could reveal a written clue that provides the group's first activity instructions.

DO IT YOURSELF

The easiest of the lot

WHAT TO DO

Not much really. Simply ask your group to split according to their own needs and wishes, into as many groups as you command. On most occasions, you will want an even number of players in each "team" so this will likely be the only boundary the group has to respect.

However, while this option is very attractive insofar as it does not involve much work on your part, I do suggest the exercise will benefit from some further boundaries of your choosing. Otherwise, you could end up with largely un-even teams (in terms of numbers, as well as expertise, experience, gender), the reinforcement of "cliques" or a group of people off to the side who are not wanted by anybody!

It's a good thing to "empower" our groups programmatically where possible, but there are times when we need to provide them with a little guidance. To help achieve a more balanced, yet random selection of team members, propose that the group-splitting process respects a set criterion, for example, an even distribution of male / female, age, background, expertise, etc.

When framed correctly, this method will work more often than not. However, if you choose to go this way, be prepared that the group may neglect your good intentions, in which case, you will have no other choice than to proceed with the groupings they create.

MAIN COURSE

This section is jam-packed full of the best and most fun activity ideas I have come across that require absolutely no equipment. From the simplest of ice-breakers to get your group started to a series of complex group problem-solving activities that will challenge your charges for an hour or so, here is a range of highly successful no prop activities for you to enjoy.

The activities have been broadly categorised according to their most common use. However, before you dive head-long into the following pages, it is useful to understand what distinguishes each type of activity from the other.

ACTIVITY GROUPING

Ice-breakers

Activities that set the tone, and invite people to interact in a non-threatening manner

- Fun and laughter is normally a major component.
- Success-oriented
- Minimal verbal and decision-making skills required

Warm-Ups & Stretches

Activities that encourage participation, and invite people to take some risks

- Success / failure are less important than trying.
- Set within cooperative and supportive atmosphere

Tag Games

Activities in which fun and action are major components

- Win / lose is less important than participation.
- Emphasis on physical movement and interaction

Trust Exercises

Activities that provide an express opportunity for group members to trust their physical and emotional safety with others

- Involves physical and verbal interaction
- Emphasis on fun, but fear as well
- Risk-taking is encouraged at many levels.

Problem-solving Initiatives

Activities that provide group members an opportunity to effectively communicate, cooperate and achieve group and individual goals together

- Involves physical and verbal interaction to solve problems
- Pooling of collective resources encouraged
- Issues of leadership, teamwork and planning are often discussed

Now, the trap many folks fall into is believing that because an activity fits into one category, it cannot be used elsewhere in your program sequence. For some activities, this may be the case, but for most, this is not a truth. A simple tweaking of a rule here, or the introduction of a limitation there, and voila, you have a new activity.

For example, consider Mute Line-Up, a wonderful old war-horse initiative that is perfect for learning about communication skills. But, with less emphasis on how people find their spot in the line, it is a fantastic and speedy method of moving people into a straight line. Or, consider the warm-up Freeze Frame. This activity is typically used to get people's bodies moving slowly, but also serves as a wonderful insight into how well a group is connected to one another.

The beauty of the activities contained within these pages is that they can be presented in so many different ways. This book presents only a common description of the game, followed by at least one or two variations. One of the biggest traps is to think that the activity can only be done one way, or that it can only be delivered the way it was presented to you. As soon as you have tried the activity – it's yours, and then with a little poetic license, you can change it however you like.

A Note on Safety

It is important to consider the safety aspects of each activity, and to address the concerns that each one presents. Remember, no-prop activities involve the same risk management concerns that prop activities do: being aware of environment, hazards and terrain, group ability, readiness, clothing and so on.

When briefing the activities in this book, point out hazards in the play area that may cause harm, such as dips in terrain. If grass is wet and slippery, be especially wary of doing running games. Issues of terrain and environment are one of the reasons that games produce more injuries than low or high challenge courses combined!

Additionally, be aware of medical and physical issues in your group that may cause a particular activity to be inappropriate. Shoulder injuries, sprained ankles and back problems are common, and can be exacerbated given the nature of some activities. Challenge by Choice is more than an essential cornerstone in program quality; it's also an important tool in keeping people safe. Make sure that participants understand their choices.

Finally, be on the look-out for group readiness. Do participants have the skills to perform the activity? Has a particular participant been shown to be somewhat unsteady on his feet? Lack of readiness can also put a group at risk. Follow the guidelines for sequencing to increase the chances of a safe experience for all.

DESCRIPTION FORMAT

Each activity is described, for the most part, using the following characteristics:

AT A GLANCE
Designed to give you a basic idea of what the activity is and looks like in one breath

WHAT YOU NEED

- General requirements of space needed to run the activity successfully and safely
- An estimate of the recommended number of people this activity is best suited for – but rarely a hard and fast rule. Maximums will be expressed if deemed necessary.
- Estimated time you can expect the activity will run for (not including the briefing, or variations)

WHAT TO DO
A play-by-play description of how you could choose to introduce the activity; everything you need to know to get you started. Much of my language will be presented as if I were speaking directly to a group, but I pull out of the group context often to put on my "trainer hat."

VARIATIONS
Suggestions from simple rule changes to complex variations of the basic activity. For most activities, the sky's the limit.

As a further guide, the illustrations aim to capture the essence or critical elements of each activity, to make it a little easier for the activities to lift off the page for you.

TWEAKING THE CHALLENGE

One of the surest ways of transforming an activity from, say an ice-breaker to a trust exercise or a group problem-solving exercise to a tag game, is to adjust the challenge. Or, within the context of an initiative, you may simply wish to make it easier or harder for a particular group.

Here are a number of variables you can use to tweak the challenge of an activity, or to help you deal with that dreaded "I've-done-this-before" syndrome. Some of these ideas come under the general heading of "rules," but some are required during the briefing of your activity.

Time: Introduce a time limit to reflect stress and real world deadlines, or remove one to assess how well the group copes with open-time lines.

Resources / Equipment / Space: Supply more or less resources which may involve information, equipment, technology and even physical space limitations.

Handicaps: Removing the use of one or more people's speech or eyesight, or ability to use certain limbs (where safe to do so).

Obstacles: Introduce pre-determined, or random obstacles which aim to impede the progress of the group, such as water, bridges, and "safe" and "unsafe" contact areas.

Scenario: Present the activity as it is (get your group from here to there in 30 minutes), as a fantasy (you have to save the pink Zulu elephants from a tribe of rampaging pygmies) or as a metaphor to reflects a number of key elements of the "real-world" for your group.

Keep in mind that the first four variables can be used as a form of penalty if you choose, perhaps wrapped in a particular scenario. For example, if you do not cross the proverbial peanut-butter pit within 30 minutes, the island you are standing on (represented by a circle of rope) will get smaller.

ICE-BREAKERS

These activities provide an opportunity for the members of your group to begin to feel comfortable with one another. Even if the people know each other pretty well, ice-breakers will always start your program off with a few laughs.

Ice-breakers typically feature:

- Fun as a major component
- Lots of non-threatening interaction
- Success-oriented activity
- Minimal verbal and decision-making skills

Whole of Group Ice-Breakers

Categories
Clumps
Gotcha
Spectrums
Psychic Handshake
Elevator Air

Partner Ice-Breakers

Paired-Shares
Partner Handshakes
Thumb Wrestling In Stereo
Wiggle Waggle
Tiny Teach

Name Games

Imaginary Toss A Name Game
Fill Me In
Me You You Me
Zombie Name Game
Name Roulette
That Ain't Me Babe!
Cocktail Party
Turbo Name Tag

All of the above

ESP
Zip Zap
Bumpity Bump Bump Bump
Zippity Bump
Impulse Names
Impulse Knees
1-2-3-4
Train Station

CATEGORIES

The perfect ice-breaker – ideal for mixing people in a fun and non-threatening manner

AT A GLANCE
Your group splits into a variety of smaller groupings, according to a series of categories you announce.

WHAT YOU NEED
An open space for a group to spread out
Minimum of 10 people
10 – 20 minutes

WHAT TO DO
Ask your group to separate according to the categories or groupings you are about to announce. For example, if the category is "colour of your pants," everyone wearing blue jeans will group together. Sometimes, individuals may find themselves alone, but in most cases, small groupings of commonality will develop. Upon identifying each of the groups, announce the next split. You can keep splitting folks for as long as they are having fun, or you run out of ideas.

For mixing purposes, alternate between two-group splits and multi-group splits. If you have the time, and the inclination, as soon as the groups have formed, give the participants a few moments to say hello to one another, or perhaps share something of relevance to the category, e.g., what was so cool about being the oldest / youngest / in-between child in your family.

Here are just a few sample group categories. There are simply hundreds of them out there, so please, don't hesitate to make up your own, or tempt them from your group.

Simple half-half splits

- Arm that ends up crossed over the top of the other, when folded on your chest
- Leg you put into your pants, shorts, underwear, etc. first when dressing
- Side of the bed you (typically) get out of in the morning (as you are lying in it, facing the ceiling)
- Position of your thumbs, that is left or right on top, when you clasp your hands together so that your fingers interlock
- Last digit of your home telephone number. All the odd numbers – 1, 3, 5, 7 or 9 – get together, and the even numbers do the same.

- When presented with a "good news / bad news story," which do you prefer to hear first?
- Preference for the way toilet paper spills off the roll – like a waterfall, over the top and forward, or against the back towards the wall.

Simple multi-group splits

- Month / zodiac sign in which you were born
- Number of siblings in your family, including yourself

- Colour of your eyes, hair, socks, etc
- Type of shoes you are wearing (not necessarily their brand)
- Type of breakfast you ate this morning
- Your favourite hot / cold beverage
- Distance you have travelled to get here {use clumps of distances, such as 0-5km, 5-10km, etc. (10 miles, 150 miles, etc.)}
- Number of items you recycle at home, e.g., glass, tin, paper, etc.

Variation

Use to divide a large group into roughly random and even teams. If you are looking for an even split, and just don't seem to find a category that fits, simply use the old scientific method of indiscriminately moving a few people ("Hey, you and you, move over here.") to even out the groupings.

CLUMPS

Zany, fast-paced energiser designed to mix people frequently

AT A GLANCE
People form groups consisting of the number called out by the instructor.

WHAT YOU NEED
A flat, open space with room to move
Minimum of 20 people
10 minutes

WHAT TO DO
This is so simple, yet so good. Gather your group around, and explain that in a moment you will shout out a number – any number from, say one to ten (the bigger your group, the bigger you can make the top end). Immediately, everyone must form a group consisting of that number of people. In my experience, groups get very huggy at this point, and form little fortresses with their bodies to prevent others from joining their little huddle.

Naturally, you will often get a few poor souls left over, the so-called remainder, if we speak in the language of long division. At this moment, you have several options. You can eliminate these folks, move them to the side, and continue with the next shouted number, and so on until you get the lucky "winners." This is cool; however, I think it's best to simply shout another number. It keeps the energy up, is much less competitive, and more fun for every-

one. And the look on the faces of the "dejected" when they hear the next number called ("I'm saved") is priceless. Move from five to three, then up to nine and back down to four so that a high degree of mixing occurs. Shout "One!" just to see what happens.

Variations

- Add the proviso that every time a new number is called, a person cannot form a new group with anyone who was in their previous group. This tweaking of the rules will spoil the plans of those crafty individuals who prefer to stick together, simply opting to ebb and flow in terms of their membership number at any point in time.

- Or, form a group according to a simple, easily-accessible category, such as dark-coloured tops, brand of running shoes, gender, colour of eyes, etc.

GOTCHA

Never fails to produce raptures of laughter

AT A GLANCE
Standing in a circle with their index fingers pointing downward into their partners' open palms, everyone tries to catch the juxta-positioned finger at the same time.

WHAT YOU NEED
An open area to form an arm's-width-apart circle
Minimum of 2 players
10 minutes

WHAT TO DO

Ask your group to form a circle, facing inwards and standing side by side. (Note, this next bit is best if you demonstrate as you explain it.) Holding your right hand out to your right hand side (about shoulder height) with your palm facing upwards, extend the index finger of your left hand, and place it into the open palm of the person on your left.

Look around, and you should all be inextricably linked. Now, on the command "Go!" – which works pretty well to start a game – everyone tries to catch the finger of the person on their right, that which is pointing downward, touching the centre of their palm. Of course, jocularity prevails, because everyone is also trying to avoid being caught by the person on their left. I just love that bit. Ask people to shout out "Gotcha!" when they catch a finger.

Now, you could try to move on, but I doubt you will want to. There are ample moments of humour here. Observe the way in which the palms of some people, which first started out as flat, are slowly curling with each round. Or the proclivity of folks to not want to touch their finger tip on their neighbour's palm, lest they get caught!! It's all so funny.

Variations

- Try this again several times, switching palms from the right to the left (to benefit our left-brained friends), i.e., the left palm is facing upwards, and a right index finger is extended.
- Cross your arms as you play, i.e., extend the right palm in front of your chest to point toward the person on your left, and place your left index finger into the waiting palm on your right.
- Try all variations with your palms upside-down, and fingers pointing up.
- Same original set-up, but add a further challenge. Instruct people to place their right foot and toes directly above, but not touching the left foot of your right-hand-side partner. On "Go," you try to tag the foot of your partner, whilst trying to avoid being tagged and performing the usual finger and palm routine.
- Everything above, but groups of only two or three or whatever.

SPECTRUMS

A passive "get to know you more" game

AT A GLANCE
People respond to a series of questions by standing between two imaginary points of a spectrum.

WHAT YOU NEED
An area as wide as your group needs to form a single line
Minimum of 12 people
15 minutes

WHAT TO DO
Create in the mind's eye of your group a sense of an imaginary line that stretches between two points – be it two walls, a couple of trees, whatever. Describe the concept of a spectrum, suggesting that if black was at one end and white the other, all the shades of grey would be in between.

Having created this metaphor, announce to your group that you would like each individual to place him or her self along this spectrum according to their responses to a series of questions and scenarios. They can choose to be anywhere along the imaginary line, but stress that it is their decision, and they should try not to be influenced by where their peers and friends are standing.

For example, explain that the spectrum represents how we, as individuals, typically view waking up in the morning. On the left-hand side of the spectrum, we have the early risers, those folks who just can't wait to get out of bed, and are pumped as soon as their feet hit the floor. Then, at the extreme right-hand side, we have those poor souls who hit the snooze button twice and need three cups of coffee to remember even what day it is. And of course, everyone else fits somewhere in between.

Upon announcing each scenario or question, ask people to move where they belong within the spectrum. There are no right or wrong answers. But the depth and breadth of the spread will reflect a number of characteristics about the group. From time to time, invite the group to observe where the group is generally situated, and perhaps even ask them to share with a few neighbours or with the larger group what this might mean. Or, of course, you could simply move people from one

black ....white

spectrum to the next solely for the purposes of mixing, getting to know one another and having fun.

Here are a few spectrums to start with, then make up a few of your own.

Variations

- Your exercise regime – never to several hours every day
- Dominant source of energy – introversion to extraversion
- Job preference – totally indoors to totally outdoors
- Car security – never lock your car to always lock your car, even if you are gone for 30 seconds
- Preferred home – deep inner city to remote wilderness
- Preparation – fully studied and prepared for anything to totally flying by the seat of your pants

PSYCHIC HANDSHAKE

A really FUNN, random method of forming a specified number of groups

AT A GLANCE
People shake hands a fixed number of times to determine the group they belong to.

WHAT YOU NEED
An open space for pairs to mingle
Minimum of 10 psychics
5 minutes

WHAT TO DO
Begin by asking everyone in your group to think of a number, and keep it to themselves. The selection of a number will be determined by the number of small groups you wish to create. So, if you want four groups at the end of this exercise, ask them to think of the numbers 1, 2, 3 or 4.

The idea is for everyone who is thinking of the same number to find each other and gather in one spot. But, unless your group has some extra sensory perceptors at work, I would suggest

they will need some further instructions to help them find their designated group. This is where the fun is.

With a number in mind, invite each person to approach another and immerse themselves in a very friendly shaking of hands. Each person will literally shake their own hand (read, arm as well) corresponding to the number they are thinking of, and so will their partner. The key to this banter is for each person to hold their arm firm when he / she accomplishes the required number of shakes. So, if you are thinking "three" and I'm thinking "two," we will happily shake one another's hands for the first two shakes, and then suddenly my arm and hand will go stiff, and prevent any further mutual shakes. At this juncture, it will be obvious from the level of grunts and laughter that emanate from you as you struggle with my "holding firm" position, that we are not on the same wave-length and belong in different groups.

It's a good idea to demonstrate what the "shaking of hands" and "holding firm" positions look like – in front of everyone before you say, "Go" – to give everyone a clue and a chance to giggle at what is really a very FUNN exchange.

Suggest to your group that it is most effective if they remain silent throughout the frenetic shaking period. That is, no talking, but laughter is permitted. Also, a few smart folks will think to indicate with their out-stretched fingers, or by clapping, the number they are thinking of. Applaud their ingenuity, but suggest that it's more fun to stick to the shaking.

Variation

Same set-up, but blind-folded.

ELEVATOR AIR

A gentle, yet experiential way to introduce the tone of your program

AT A GLANCE
People cross to the other side of the circle in which they are standing in the manner of being in an elevator.

WHAT YOU NEED
A flat, open area to accommodate a wide circle
Minimum of 10 people
5 – 10 minutes

WHAT TO DO
Everyone knows what it means to be in an elevator. You step in. No one looks at you. You press the button for your floor. Doors close, and you instinctively glance up at the numbers blinking above the doors as if you've forgotten how to count. Moments pass, you glance up again and can't believe that you still have ten floors to go. You can't wait to get out… you know how it goes.

Share a little of this with your group, to get them ready for what's next. It will often spark a chortle or two, perhaps even a few comments about how dumb this all seems. If this happens, it is just perfect, and I recommend you allow it to occur.

Starting in a large circle, invite every person to simply walk to the other side of the circle from where they are standing as if they had just entered an elevator. No talking, barely any eye contact, and certainly no interaction. Take note of what happens, how it feels, etc.

Ask everyone to return to their original spots in the circle, this time as if they were entering a room full of people they knew and were comfortable with. Again, observe what happens. Without even saying it, I can guarantee they will instinctively go out of their way to interact with one another.

Now, ask the group: Which atmosphere felt the most comfortable? Which atmosphere do you believe would be the most productive? You can probably see where this is heading, right? Take just a few moments to establish what caused the difference, and to connect this to your program. Typically, comments such as "It was safer," "I felt trusted," "I knew everyone better," "I was able to take risks" will be offered. Fantastic! Suggest that this is exactly what you hope to achieve with your program. Invite every member of your group to take responsibility for creating this atmosphere right here, right now. You're ready to move on.

Variation

Add one further crossing in the manner of walking into a wild party. Discussion can still follow focusing on the impact of "being" this way with people.

PAIRED-SHARES

Classic technique to break the ice and generate energy and discovery

AT A GLANCE
People share their responses to a series of questions with a partner or partners.

WHAT YOU NEED
An area comfortable for pairs to stand or sit in conversation
Whatever people you have
10 – 20 minutes

WHAT TO DO
It's as simple as breaking your group into pairs, and tossing a few questions their way to invite the partners to share. Start slowly with a series of fun, non-threatening questions, and then build up the challenge to more personal, revealing questions.

I prefer to start with two people in a group in the beginning because it's pretty hard to be left out of a pair. Groups of three or four are fine, but there is still the chance someone may be left out, or ignored, and this may run counter to your objectives.

Also, it's a good idea to ask people to move about between each question or two, so that they get to meet and learn something about more people in the group. To avoid people picking their friends all the time, use a variety of techniques to guide the selection of partners, such as someone:

• with similar colour eyes, top, hair, etc.
• born in the same month
• wearing same size shoe
• who is also the oldest, youngest or in-between in the family.

The following list of questions is by no means exhaustive, but it will give you a few starting points:

Your favourite cartoon or TV show?

Your most annoying driving habit?

The best electronic game you own?

Name one or more talents / skills you wish you had.

Naughtiest thing you did when you were young?

Your most memorable adventure experience.

Name a person – dead or alive – you would like to meet for dinner.

Name three of your most important values.

If you were 20 years old again, what would you do differently?

If you could ask God just one question, what would it be?

Describe the best kiss you ever had.

If you could be invisible for one hour, what would you do?

If you could eliminate one hereditary characteristic from your family, what would it be?

Variations

- Divide into groups of three or four.
- Invite suggestions of questions to ask.

PARTNER HANDSHAKES

High energy, terribly playful get-to-know-you activity

AT A GLANCE
People engage in a series of culturally ambiguous greetings with others.

WHAT YOU NEED
A flat, open space for mingling
Minimum of 10
5 – 10 minutes

WHAT TO DO
Have the group spread out. Invite them to approach as many members of the group as possible, engaging in a cultural greeting of sorts in accordance with your instructions. Try to introduce about five or six quick, distinct, yet culturally ambiguous greetings, each one inviting a little more "risk" (read "silliness") than the one before it.

Here are a few examples, presented in a sequence which demonstrates a progression of sorts. Where communication exists, encourage people to use the other person's name.

Passer-by – a slight nod of the head as you walk by someone, which says "I-see-you-there-but-don't-wish-to-talk-to-you."

Secret admirer – a smile and a wink of the eye, perhaps a turn of your head, as you pass by that person.

English person – take off your hat and nod acknowledgement of the other as you pass them.

Aussie – smile and say "G'day mate in your best "ocker" accent as you pass by.

Yankee doodle dandy – go right up to someone, shake their hands, and say "How ya doin'?" in your best American drawl.

Japanese doll – stand in front of your partner, bow and say something appropriately Japanese, such as "Yamaha," "Mitsubishi" or "Fujitsu."

Sumo wrestler – puff yourself up, push your tummy out and walk as if your legs were made of lead balloons, and bounce off the tummy of another Sumo wrestler.

Babylonian – back up to your partner, bend forward, and poke your hand back and through your legs to shake the hand of your partner doing the same thing.

French – press your lips against..... ummm, only kidding!

Variation

Develop all manner of themes to your greetings, allowing each level to get progressively more difficult / fun. For example, if you re working with children, develop a series of greetings for fish starting from the little minnows to whales.

THUMB WRESTLING IN STEREO

Fantastic variation on an old favourite

AT A GLANCE
Partners form a monkey grip with their hands, and each tries to pin the other person's thumb under their own first.

WHAT YOU NEED
An open space for pairs to mingle
At least 2 wrestlers
10 minutes

WHAT TO DO
Ask your group to separate into pairs. Using the same hand, instruct each person to hold their partner's hand as if in the typical "monkey's grip" position, i.e., fingers curled into the palm of the other. At this juncture, you could simply launch into wrestle mania, but try these two fun adaptations to add a little pizzazz to an otherwise I-can-see-what's-going-to-happen activity:

1. Ask each person to grasp the free hand of their partner to form a second "combat zone" situated on top of or below their already coupled hands. Their arms should now looked crossed, to give that peculiar stereo look.

2. Suggest that before play commences, the partners should join in a quick preparative ditty of "One,

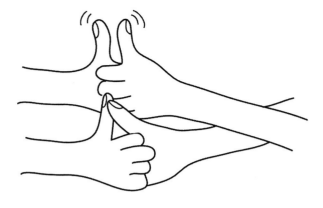

two, three, four; I declare a thumb war," during which the opposing thumbs alternate side to side across their respective corners of the "playing field."

You are now primed to engage in mortal thumb combat. The object is to pin your partner's thumb under your own first.

Note: Slipping out from under your partner's thumb, after having been momentarily pinned, is a breach of the international thumb wrestling rules! Let the games begin.

Variations

- Swap the set of hands that appears on top of the other.
- Try it with three or four people. Continue to apply the "monkey's grip" posture, but this time all wrestlers curl their fingers in one big clump of palm propinquity. Opportunities to form alliances (i.e., "Let's work together to pin HIS thumb first.") adds another level of excitement to the game.

WIGGLE WAGGLE

An old school yard illusion that's just plain FUNN

AT A GLANCE
A person clasps their hands as if in prayer, and then twists their hands and fingers to create a fun illusion.

WHAT YOU NEED
An open space for pairs to gather
As many wagglers as you can muster
10 minutes

WHAT TO DO
This is one of those activities that truly relies on a good demonstration, or illustration to fully comprehend how it's done. Even then, some people won't be able to get it right away. Encourage them to just enjoy the process and keep trying for as long as their patience lasts.

Start by pressing the palms and fingers of your two hands together in a prayer like form just in front of your chest. Notice that as your hands are pressed against each other, it's as if there were a thin sheet of glass separating them. Keep this image in mind.

Look at the middle fingers of both your hands – they are often the tallest fingers, which is good. Take your left middle finger and slide it physically past the right middle finger, so that from your point of view, it passes behind the right middle finger. Let the left middle finger fall (or point down) at right angles to the rest of the fingers. As a consequence, the right middle finger can do the same.

That was the easy part. The trick is to imagine that other than your two middle fingers, every other finger is about to slide across the imagined sheet of glass that rests between your hands. This image is critical because you are likely to break a finger in this next step otherwise. While in the prayer position, and while keeping your left hand still, move your right hand away from your body until you have moved your hand 180 degrees from your starting point. As you do this complex little slide action, you must prevent all of your other fingers from wandering into enemy territory and falling in behind the fingers of the other hand.

You know you have finished because as you look down at your hands, you will see, your right middle finger pointing up at you, with your left palm facing down, partly obscuring your right palm facing up. Your left middle finger is underneath pointing down towards the ground. Phew, you've done it!

Now, practice a few times, and get ready for the fun. Find yourself a partner, and face them about a metre (40

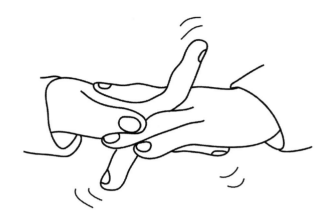

inches) or so apart. Look them dead in the eye, with daggers (you should ham this up big time). Place your arms just out from your sides, twitching nervously with that Clint Eastwood "make my day" look about you. On the word "Go," the first person to perform a wiggle waggle wins!

It's that easy – not!! But it's sure to bring howls of laughter. Best way to conduct this activity is to encourage people to mingle about the area, and as soon as you spot another person not "dueling," get their attention, square up to them, give them the eye, aaannnndddd, go!

Variations

- Slide your left middle finger to the front side of your right middle finger. This will cause you to slide your palms and hands in the other direction. Ideal for the already adept wiggle waggler.
- Form a circle, and set your arms and palms in the direction of your two partners. Place a palm each against your left and right partners' palms, and... um, you can guess the rest. Once you've given your group a few moments to test this new technique, time how long it takes from the arms down position to achieve a full group wiggle waggle.

TINY TEACH

A series of quick, paired activities that are fun and teachable

AT A GLANCE
People demonstrate a series of simple skills and teach them to a partner.

WHAT YOU NEED
An open area in which to mingle
Minimum of 8 tiny teachers
5 to 15 minutes

WHAT TO DO
Split your group into pairs, and explain that you will announce a series of quick partner activities. You can choose to introduce one exercise and then invite people to swap partners. Or, even better, choose to have the partners break up and "teach" what they have just learned to a new partner.

Here are some suggestions. Keep in mind, the emphasis is on the trying not the accomplishment.

- **Tie a pair of shoe-laces:** Each partner unties the laces of the shoe closest to their partner as they stand side-by-side. The object is for each person, using only one hand each, to tie the shoe laces (one from each shoe) together with a standard bow. If only one person has shoes, same exercise, just re-tie the one shoe lace.

- **Whistle:** You'll be amazed at how many people cannot whistle. This exercise is about teaching one another how to do it. The delightful chorus of hollow breaths and chuckles is worth all the trying.

- **Whistle into your hands:** Cup your hands tightly together to form an "air-tight" container, all but for a small gap in the top between your thumbs. Blow over the top of this hole, and you will make a hollow-pitched whistling sound. You will. Just keep trying.

- **Tell a Joke:** Hands up if you have trouble remembering a joke? No matter how long or short, funny or

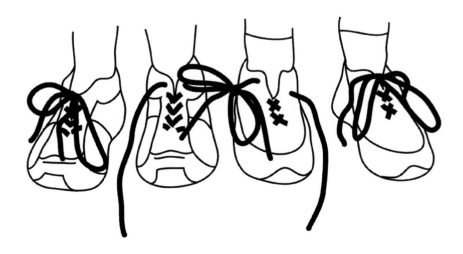

not, pass on a favourite joke to your partner. Come on, everyone can think of at least one joke!

- **Let Me Show You:** This is completely open. Each person presents any little skill or talent they choose to their partner. The choices are endless – stuff like how to curl your tongue, how to sing, how to do a simple yoga move and sharing a pub trick are all examples of what I've seen folks pull out of their hats.

- **Body Gym:** This tiny teach never ceases to amaze me for its sheer inventiveness. Partners take turns showing and then teaching how to do something completely bizarre with their bodies. Dislocating their shoulder, rolling their eyes back, bending over backwards and touching the floor, twisting their hand a full 720 degrees around (and not screaming!), are all examples of what I have seen people do. We are all, indeed, completely out of the ordinary.

Variation

Add Thumb Wrestling in Stereo and Wiggle Waggle to your "teachable" repertoire.

IMAGINARY TOSS A NAME GAME

Excellent name game, just like the real thing, but without the tossables

AT A GLANCE
People stand in a circle passing imaginary items to each other as they call and learn each other's names.

WHAT YOU NEED
An open area
Minimum of 10 tossers
10 – 20 minutes

WHAT TO DO
This works pretty much like the golden oldie "Toss a Name Game" as found in many of Project Adventure's earlier titles, but without props of course!

Form a square without sides, and pull an imaginary ball from your pocket. As you demonstrate your sporting prowess with this ball, toss it about, juggle it, and balance it on your nose – you get the idea. The trick is, will your group? It's all about having fun.

To begin, pass the "ball" around the circle, from left to right. Each person calls out their name clearly when they receive the ball. This may be the first time the group has heard everyone's names. Pass the ball back the other way, and repeat the process, but this time ask that people remember at least one other person's name before it gets back to the start (often you!). Now the fun begins.

Whoever has the ball now, is entitled to toss it (notice I said toss, and not zing!!) to anyone in the circle, but must first call that person's name. Their attention is attracted, they anxiously await the toss, and voila! it's received. Nice pass. The process continues.

At some point, interrupt the tossing, and suggest that the tossable is no longer a ball – it has turned into something else, a watermelon, perchance. So, from now on, all future passes will reflect the weight and size of a watermelon, or whatever object it is deemed to be. A little later, transform the tossable again, this time into a shot-put. Soon enough, invite whoever has the item to decide what it is they are tossing. An exchange could sound like this, for example, "Terry, it's a balloon, catch!" Terry responds, "Hey Barbara, it's no longer a balloon. It's a basketball," and so on.

As a general level of name-knowingness develops, introduce more "items" into the circle. There could be four items being tossed by different people at the same time. Chaos will hold sway, but don't worry too much. People will be having fun, and learning names in the process.

Eventually, throw down the gauntlet, and challenge one or more folks to name as many people in the group as possible (notice, I didn't say "name everyone"). No matter how big the group is, there is always one person who will give it a go.

Variations

- Ask the people who receive an item to say "thank you" to the person who tossed it to them, but most importantly, using that person's name.
- An ideal twist for folks who have trouble remembering names – interrupt the game, and revert to one tossable again. This time, the tosser will receive eye contact from the person to whom they wish to pass, but does not call his / her name. Instead, as the person receives the pass, everyone in the circle calls out the receiver's name. In that way, a player could deliberately pass the item to someone he or she doesn't know, mime a couple of words (to make it look good) and listen carefully as the group calls out the correct name. Remember, it's all about how you look!

FILL ME IN

A name reminder game featuring a chaotic combination of movements

AT A GLANCE
People assume the place of a person standing in the circle whose name they have just called.

WHAT YOU NEED
A flat, open space
Minimum of 10, and up to 30, more if your group has a good level of name-knowingness
10 – 15 minutes

WHAT TO DO
Having formed a circle, the action begins when one person steps into the circle – at the same time announcing the name of someone who is on the other side of the circle from them – and walks toward that person. The first person fills the space of the newly announced person as this second person moves into the centre of the circle and immediately calls out a third person's name, and the process starts all over again.

In and out, in and out it goes. When you believe the group is ready for more, introduce a second and third person calling out a name across the circle. A series of chaotic and confusing crossings will result. At this time, encourage lots of eye contact and careful movements.

Variations

- Invite the person who has called out a name, to introduce themselves by name to the other. Perhaps shake hands before this other person repeats the process.
- As the movement of people in the centre of the circle gains momentum, invite people to shake hands and greet (using the name) someone as they pass them in the middle of the circle.

ME YOU YOU ME

Simplest "know your name" game, that is just oh so hard

AT A GLANCE
Walking around the circle, each person introduces his or her name and repeats the name of every other person one at a time.

WHAT YOU NEED
An open area to form a circle
Minimum of 6, but not more than 20 people
10 minutes

WHAT TO DO
Start with a circle. Using your example as a demonstration, step in front of the person who was standing to your left. Shake this person's hand, and simply say your own name. Nothing else, no "How do you do", or "My name is…," simply state your name. Whilst still shaking hands, your partner will now say his or her name. Pretty easy so far, but it's not over. Here comes the hard part.

The person who first introduced him or her self (you in the case of the demonstration), now repeats back the name of the person they are greeting (you're still shaking hands by the way). Again, nothing more, just repeat their name. And your partner repeats your name back to you. Phew, it's over, you can unclasp sweaty hands, and move on to the next person, to your right in the circle. So, if I was starting, and your name was Susan, our exchange would sound like this – "Mark, *Susan*, Susan, *Mark*".

The process continues with each greeter moving to their right (on the inside of the circle), allowing the person next in line to fall in behind them to greet the person the first greeter has

just greeted – just like a snake, get it? Each person will walk on the inside of the circle and greet everyone once, and then resume their original position in the circle, and then have every other person greet them a second time as these folks return to their original spot.

It really is very simple. It's just not easy. And I can almost guarantee you, inside the time it takes for the first few exchanges, the group will erupt in guffaws as one or more people mix up their names. It's astonishing how often people "use" the wrong name at the wrong time. This is a classic in the making.

Variations

- Exchange the use of a name with something interesting about yourself, e.g., honest, fun, thirty-two, Brazilian, etc. That was not meant to sound like a personal ad, but you get the idea.
- Instead of shaking hands, bow and say the person's name Japanese style.

ZOMBIE NAME GAME

Zany, interactive name-reminder game

AT A GLANCE
Upon hearing his or her name called out, a player must call out the name of another person who is standing in the circle, before they are tagged by the "zombie."

WHAT YOU NEED
A flat, open space for a circle to form
About 10, and up to 40 potential zombies with a good level of name-knowingness
10 – 15 minutes

WHAT TO DO
Start your group in a circle, and playing full-out to demonstrate what you are looking for, walk forward into the centre of the circle with your arms stretched out in front of you "zombie" like, almost as if you were sleep-walking, hands dangling at the end of your arms.

As you leave your spot, call out the name of a person standing on the other side of the circle from you. Your object as the "zombie" is to tag the person you have nominated before they get a chance to quickly call out the name of another person standing in the circle, i.e., not your name or their name, but someone else's. Make it look like you are a zombie, and are about to throttle this other person's throat – which of course you do not. Suggest that if contact is inevitable, a compassionate tag on the shoulders with both hands is all that is required. Also, in the interests of safety and fair-play, suggest that the zombies keep to a brisk walk at most.

If the person about to be "zombied" (ah, that's a much better term than "throttled") manages to call out a name before they get tagged, the newly-named person immediately leaves their spot in the circle. This spot

is assumed by the first zombie, and the new zombie repeats the process, i.e., they walk with out-stretched arms and walk across to the person whose name they have just called. And so it goes.

Watch the terror on people's faces as they suddenly become aware that they are about to be zombied. As if they had no time to think of a name before this moment, right? It's hilarious.

So what happens if the zombie "tags" someone too slow to blurt out a name? Well, you have a few options. You could simply ask the person who was zombied to stand out of the circle, and continue with the game as successive zombies eliminate everyone. However, I prefer to keep everyone "in," and suggest that if someone is too slow, or blurts out a wrong name, they simply assume the role of the zombie, and play on.

Variations

- Introduce second, third and fourth zombies into the action.
- With a large group, suggest to the zombies they may travel a little faster, but keeping an eye to collisions at all times.
- Give people three chances (or lives) before they are eliminated from the circle (in this case, quit the game soon after the energy reaches its peak, regardless of the number of eliminations – otherwise, you could bore people to death!).

NAME ROULETTE

A name-reminder game with a casino-esque plot

AT A GLANCE
Two circles of people holding hands rotate directly next to each other. When "Stop!" is called, the person from each circle who is closest to a designated spot, will attempt to call out the name of the other first.

WHAT YOU NEED
Flat, open space, large enough for two circles
Minimum of 20, and up to 60 relatively active folks with a good level of name-knowingness
10 – 15 minutes

WHAT TO DO
Split your gathering into two relatively even groups, and ask each of them to form a circle by holding hands with their partners, facing into the centre. The two circles are not physically linked, but the outside edges of each circle will meet at a designated spot. It is useful to identify this spot – such as the centre circle of a basketball court, or a chalk mark, whatever – but it's not critical. Each group just needs to understand that one edge of its circle must pass by this spot at all times.

You then ask each circle to rotate, keeping a hold of their partners' hands. It does not matter which direction they travel, but they should travel at an even speed that is comfortable for the least able in the group. From a bird's eye view, it should look as if two circles are spinning and their edges at the closest

point are about a metre (40 inches) apart, passing over the designated spot.

Now, come in Spinner. At a time of your choosing, find a way to squeeze into the gap between the two rotating circles, and tap the shoulders of the two people (one from each circle) who are right now passing over the "spot." Everyone else will see this occur, will stop moving, and as quickly as possible, the two tapped people must turn around and try to call the name of the other before they get named. It's fast, high on energy, and you could get dizzy, but it's fun.

From this point, you have at least two options. You could award points to the group when one of its members correctly calls out the name of the other. Or, you could reward this group by "winning" that other person to join their circle, i.e., your circle gets bigger with every win.

Keep an eye on the speed of the circles. It doesn't take much to whip people around the circle out of excitement, and then you have a real lottery on your hands.

Variations

- Ask your groups to form a circle by facing out, rather than into the circle.
- Play music, then turn it off (think musical chairs) to indicate when the circles have to stop, to identify which two people are closest to the spot.

THAT AIN'T ME BABE!

A "get to know you" with a difference

AT A GLANCE
A person mimes a series of interesting things about themselves to their partner, who then attempts to formally introduce this person to the group.

WHAT YOU NEED
An open space for pairs to spread out
Minimum of 10 babes
15 minutes

WHAT TO DO
Separate your group into pairs. Explain that each person will take their turn and mime (i.e., no verbal communication) three things about themselves to their partner, with a view to communi-cating enough information so their partner will be able to introduce them to the rest of the group. The trick is, neither partner can talk during this process, nor can a person repeat their mime. The mimer and observer get just one go, say about two minutes at the most, to communicate their "story."

You could choose to leave it completely open as to the choice of what a person may mime to their partner, and therefore have introduced to the group. However, if you feel that some people may struggle for ideas, or worse, choose inappropriate ones, here are a few suggestions which are typically fun to mime:

- Past occupation or part-time job
- Where you live
- A frightening experience
- Favourite movie or TV show

Once everyone has had their turn, invite each person to introduce their partner, verbalizing their interpretation of the mimes. The results are often hilarious, with many an embarrassed pronouncement of "that ain't me babe!" It's not about getting it right, although many people will. It's about creating a safe environment in which to laugh and play, as well as learning about each other, all of which will gradually build trust.

Variations

- Ask each person to mime an interesting or funny scene from their life.
- A more challenging task, invite the observing partner to mime what they saw back to the group, and ask the group to guess what it is they are communicating.

COCKTAIL PARTY

A quick name reinforcer, and welcome segue to a drinks break

AT A GLANCE
People mingle about shaking hands and greeting people by name as quickly as possible.

WHAT YOU NEED
A flat, open space for mingling
As many party-goers as you can muster
2 minutes

WHAT TO DO
Looking for a quick way to wrap up a session, perhaps reinforce a few names people may have just learned, and introduce a drinks break? This is it.

Invite people to bunch around you, capturing the image of palatial sur-roundings, evening gowns, black ties and cocktails. Suggest that each person holds in their left hand an imaginary drink, or cocktail if they choose. Then, on your signal, everyone is encouraged to meet, shake the hands of and greet as many people at the party as possible, in say, 43.5 seconds (this is not a magic number!).

On "Go," it will sound something like, "Oooohh, darling, so good to see you!. I'm having a frightfully good time.....". Chat for a few moments, discuss drinks, recent holidays to the Swiss Alps, and then in typical cocktail party fashion, interrupt the conversation with a "O, Petal, must keep moving." Air kiss, kiss

(these are not mandatory), and "...Bye bye!"...off you go to greet another party guest.

Suggest to your group that they should use the other person's name as often as possible, enquire about the other person's drink (remember, they are holding on to it), but not spend too long with any one person. For a bit of fun, ask someone for the time and see if they spill their drink!

When you feel like the heat has started to dissipate from the party, quell the action and ask your group what is odd about this activity. Someone usually will remark that "There are no drinks in their hands," which is your cue to say...."Let's remedy that situation – time for a break."

Variation

Imagine you are in a swanky Food Hall. Invite people to mingle as they treat themselves to the extraordinary array of fine foods available on people's trays.

TURBO NAME TAG

A name game, tag and problem solving activity all in one

AT A GLANCE
Bunched together, people keep their eyes closed until someone taps them on the shoulder to signal that they should quickly open their eyes to identify a new person calling their name and tapping them on the shoulder. Repeat the process until everyone has been identified.

WHAT YOU NEED
A flat, open space
Minimum of 10 people, with a good level of name-knowingness
A watch, or time-piece with a second hand
5 – 10 minutes

WHAT TO DO
Issue your group blind-folds, or better still, just ask people to keep their eyes closed for what will likely be about one to two minutes. Ask them to bunch together, with enough room for everyone to comfortably mingle about one another. Once your group has plunged into darkness, invite them to move about the area slowly, perhaps with their hands raised in front of their chests, palms facing forward, to prevent any embarrassing bumping-intos.

Upon mixing themselves adequately, ask everyone to stop where they are standing, drop their "bumpers" to their sides and keep their eyes closed. You then approach one person at random and tap them on the shoulders, and simultaneously start your stopwatch. The person you tap immediately opens his or her eyes, and moves toward any other person whom they

can identify, tapping this new person on the shoulder and calling out their name to start the process over again. A tap on the shoulder of someone who has not been "named" – either at all, or incorrectly – will result in an unofficial time, and a do-over. Observe how the imposition of a timed event causes ripples of anxiety as people struggle to name folks they have known for years.

Once a person has been tagged and subsequently passed the tap on, they can either crouch down in position, or remove themselves from the group. The key is that only those folks who have not been tapped or called remain standing. As the last person is tagged, stop the watch, and announce the time. Repeat the activity several times to achieve that nominal "world record."

Variations

- The same person (nominated before you begin) starts the name calling / tagging at every round.
- Rather than move, ask the just-been-tagged to simply call the name of a person they see to keep the ball rolling.

ESP

A mind-reading exercise that's full of fun and surprises

AT A GLANCE
Starting back to back, pairs turn around to face their partner and physically demonstrate one of several gestures, aiming to match their partner's gesture.

WHAT YOU NEED
An open space for pairs to spread out
Minimum of 8 psychics
15 minutes

WHAT TO DO
Break your group into pairs and then conduct a whole group discussion that will result in an agreement of three definable, distinct physical gestures. Your program goals will dictate what style of gestures they will be; for example, a recreational program may settle with three popular sporting movements such as a golf swing, swimming and horse-riding (to save space, you'll just have to imagine what these movements look like). Alternatively, for programs of a more intrinsic nature, you could come up with happy, sad and shocked featuring commonly accepted gestures for each of them. It doesn't matter too much, but I encourage you to motivate the group to develop the gestures, with you as the final arbiter of what is appropriate, of course!

Next, practice these gestures a few

times to ensure that everyone has got them locked in. Now ask each of the pairs to find a little space to play, and stand back to back with their partner, i.e., so that they can't see each other. Whilst waiting for the countdown, each person is silently deciding which of the three gestures he or she will choose to do. No talking or giving of clues is permitted during this period. Then, on the count of three, each person turns around swiftly to face their partner whilst demonstrating / performing one of the three gestures. A clue – instruct people to be gesturing as they turn around, to prevent a little sneaky cheating. The object of each pair is to match gestures, e.g., a swimmer faces another swimmer. Strangely, wild screams of delight emanate from the pairs regardless of whether they match or not.

Repeat this procedure five or six times, suggesting that each partnership record their own results. Upon the final round, survey your group for the most perceptive couples! It's not rare to find some partnerships earn a perfect record, but certainly not common. What does this mean? Hmmm, I'll leave that to your debrief, but a high degree of success among many of the pairs may reflect a high level of connectedness within the group. Or just plain luck!

Variations

- Try groups of three people, tougher to match, but same deal.
- Introduce four or perhaps even five distinct gestures.
- Use as a fun way to introduce an important component of your program, for example, the Full Value Contract where you facilitate the group to create a distinct physical gesture for each of the elements of agreement.

ZIP ZAP

Great energiser to develop focus and lightning fast reactions

AT A GLANCE
People standing in the circle will respond to the middle person pointing at them by either ducking or "zapping" their neighbours as fast as they can.

WHAT YOU NEED
Open flat area for a circle to form
10 minutes
Minimum of 10 and up to 40 zappers

WHAT TO DO
Stand in the centre of a circle, with your group facing toward you. Approach someone in the circle, look them straight in the eye and say "Zip." At the same time, press your two hands together with fingers pointing forward towards this person. Hint – it's a good idea for this action not to look like a gun.

As soon as you call "Zip," the person you have pointed to must duck down. This action causes his / her two neighbours to face in towards the ducker. Make up some funny physical gesture

and shout "Zap" as a response to the "Zip."

If the ducker and Zappers respond quickly, without delay or error, they each survive to play another round. However, if the ducker doesn't duck quickly enough, or one of the two Zappers doesn't "Zap" correctly or quickly enough (according to agreed zapping etiquette), the slowest or most deserving of them is invited to swap with the "Zipper" and have some fun in the middle.

Once your group "gets" what's happening, introduce one or more new zippers into the middle to ramp up the energy and fun.

Variations

- Introduce the activity as an elimination, whereby the Zipper remains in the centre of the circle all the time, and continues zipping until the final two people are left standing.
- A step further on from the above variation. Ask those folks who are eliminated to remain in the circle, but squatted down. The game continues as if they were not there, but the gap between people who are still "in" will cause some of them to overlook who their neighbours truly are, i.e., the next "in" person could be standing half way around the circle.

BUMPITY BUMP BUMP BUMP

One of the funniest name-reminder games I know

AT A GLANCE
Standing in a circle, a person will call out the name of the person to their left, right or in front of them or their own name as quickly as possible upon the instruction of the person in the middle.

WHAT YOU NEED
An open space to accommodate a circle
Minimum of 8 people
10 minutes

WHAT TO DO
Having formed your group into a circle, ask them to repeat after you the words "bumpity bump bump bump." I tend to give it a bit of a groove as I say it to impress on my groups that this is very serious stuff – not!

Explain that the person standing in the middle of the circle (in this case, you) will approach anyone in the circle, look them straight in the eye, point to them and exclaim the words "left," "right," "you" or "me." This is an instruction to call out the name of the person to their left or right, their own name, or the name of the person doing the pointing. At this juncture, I typically suggest that everyone should review the names of their neighbours, not to mention mine (the pointer) and of course their own – you'll be surprised by how few people actually choose to practice saying their own name; and they wonder why they stumble with it later!!

Anyway, to this moment, the game works fine as a name-reminder activity, but it's got no spunk. So this is where the bumps come in. To give the exercise a little edge, the person being pointed to must attempt to (correctly) name the left-right-you-or-me person as quickly as possible, indeed, before the pointer can say the words "bumpity bump bump bump." So, it looks like this – the pointer points and calls out, "Left," and immediately will follow with the groove of "bumpity bump bump bump." Meanwhile, the pointee will attempt to blurt out a name before the pointer gleefully gets to the final bump.

If the pointee manages to shout out (note, that most people confuse volume with speed in this activity) the correct name before the last bump, the pointer hangs his or her head low and moves onto another target. However, if the pointee is too slow, gives the wrong name, or simply looks like a doe in headlights, everyone has a good laugh, and the pointer and pointee swap positions.

Once your group "gets" what's happening, introduce one or more new pointers into the middle to ramp up the energy and fun.

Variations

- For younger groups, or those with lesser name-retention abilities, limit the pointer to asking for the names of "left" and "right" neighbours.
- Add, or substitute the command with "two to your left" or "three to your right" to really challenge your group.
- Choosing to play for keeps, you could choose to eliminate people as they make mistakes on their journey to the much celebrated name-knowing heaven. Even better, ask those folks who are eliminated to remain in the circle, but squatted down. The game continues as if they were not there, but the gap between people who are still "in" will cause some of them to overlook who their neighbours truly are, i.e., the next "left" or "right" person could be standing half way around the circle.

ZIPPITY BUMP

A crazy convergence of Zip Zap and Bumpity Bump Bump Bump

AT A GLANCE
Standing in a circle, the group plays Zip Zap and Bumpity Bump Bump Bump simultaneously.

WHAT YOU NEED
An open area to accommodate a circle
Minimum of 8 people
10 minutes

WHAT TO DO
First up, you need to play the aforementioned activities Zip Zap and Bumpity Bump Bump Bump – doesn't matter in what order, or how far apart, as long as your group is familiar with the games. They each have a similar set up and objectives, and when combined, make for some crazy times.

Explain now that the person in the middle of the circle can approach anyone and say "Zip," or "Left," "Right," "You" or "Me." This person is both the zipper and the pointer, now affectionately referred to as the "zippointer." Which means of course, you have to be really sharp to survive.

Again, as your group starts to grasp what's going on, introduce one or more new "zippointers" into the middle of the circle. Organised chaos? You bet. Good luck!

Variations

- There are several games that exhibit this "someone-points-and-you-have-to-do-this-quickly" type of activity. Mix and match with some of your favourites and see what happens.
- Start with two people in the middle, assigning one to be the "zipper" and the other the "pointer" all the time. When someone makes an error, this person assumes the same role (i.e., game) as caused them to be in the middle.

IMPULSE NAMES

A quick energiser featuring dubious name-reminder qualities

AT A GLANCE
Everyone situated in a circle calls out their name as quickly as possible, one after the other.

WHAT YOU NEED
An open area to accommodate a circle
Minimum of 10 impulsers
5 – 10 minutes

WHAT TO DO
For something new, ask your group to form a circle! They can be seated or standing, it's up to you, but I like the sitting-cross-legged position. Ask everyone in the circle to simply say their own name outloud a few times, a practice so to speak.

Starting with the person to your left (or right), ask them to say their name as quickly as possible as soon as you give the signal (i.e., when you say, "Go", or "1, 2, 3," for example). Then, the person to the first person's left will say his or her name, and then the next person, and around the circle the "impulse" will travel. The impulse will end with you saying your name. OK, got that? Good, because now we're going to time it.

Label the first attempts as belonging to the "A-team,' that which accepts the impulse in a clock-wise direction. Tally your results, encouraging the group to record even faster times with each round. Before too long, the impulse will sound like one very long blurted name. It's fun.

Now, for a bit more fun, send the impulse in the other direction, and label all attempts travelling this way as belonging to the "B-team." Naturally, everyone is on both teams, but something happens when you talk of pitting one team against another that stirs the competitive juices of a group. People lose sight of the reality. Of course, after several rounds for the B-team, and perhaps a few semi-finals, announce which team won!

It's unlikely that this helped anyone learn a few names, but gee it was fun.

Variations

- Send the impulse of a yell – a blood curdling, scream-at-the-top-of-your-lungs yell – around the circle. No need to time this event, nor scream anything in particular such as your name. Just simply watch and bask in the excitement, and discomfiture of people preparing for and executing their hollers. It's just not something we typically to do in front of people, so beware – this variation of Impulse is less an ice-breaker, and more a de-inhibitizer / trust exercise.
- Send something other than your name around the circle, perhaps a personal

IMPULSE KNEES

A quick "touchy-feely" energiser

AT A GLANCE
Everyone seated in a circle attempts to slap their hands on their neighbour's knees in sequence of an impulse.

WHAT YOU NEED
A comfortable area in which to seat a circle
Minimum of 10 impulsers
5 – 10 minutes

WHAT TO DO
Seat your group in a way that brings everyone's legs right up next to their neighbours. They can be in seats or sitting cross-legged on the floor, so long as their legs are visible.

Tricking people into thinking I'm about to introduce a séance, I ask my group to hold their arms out in front of them, palms facing down. Next, I instruct them to place their left palm gently onto the right knee of their left-hand side neighbour, and place their right palm onto the left knee of their right-hand side neighbour. Each person should have the palm of their neighbour resting on their knees. Get that? There should be a bevy of crossed arms as you look about.

Now, starting with your own left hand, gently tap the knee on which it rests. This triggers an impulse, which is passed to the left causing the very next hand in sequence (of knees) to tap, and then the next, and the next, and so on. Here's where it gets tricky. The impulse is created by tapping the knees in succession, not your hands. Indeed, there should be two taps (the hands of your neighbours tapping your knees) between a tap of your right hand and that of your left hand.

Send the impulse around the circle a few times, and then change directions. And for something really cool, send the

impulse in both directions at the same time, by simultaneously tapping both of your neighbour's knees. The impulses will have to cross somewhere near the half-way point of the circle, and the looks on the faces of those involved as they struggle to tap in sequence is priceless.

Variations

- Do this activity standing up. Note, while this version is totally possible, I find that after about two minutes my back gets tired leaning over my knees, and I'm not the only one.
- Invite people to sit around a large table, or lie on the floor, and create the same cross-armed formation with palms face down onto the table top or floor. Works a treat, and minimises the discomfort some people may have about being touched by others.
- Add a further twist. When someone taps his or her hand two-times in rapid succession – tap-tap – the direction of the impulse reverses. For elimination purposes, if someone taps in error (i.e., maybe they anticipated the direction would not change, but it did), that person will remove their hand from the

1-2-3-4

Fast-paced counting game that will frustrate the heck out of you

AT A GLANCE
Groups of three people extend as many fingers on one hand at the same time, to produce a total of eleven fingers.

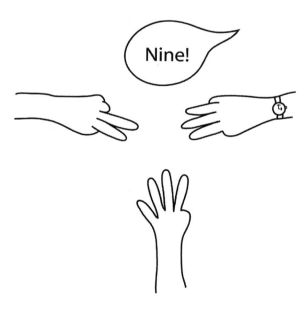

WHAT YOU NEED
An open space for people to mingle
Minimum of 3 mathematicians
5 – 10 minutes

WHAT TO DO
Break into groups of three people, facing each other. Each person extends one of their hands (it doesn't matter which one) in a clenched fist in front of the others. Shaking their fists up and down at the same time, ask your groups to chant "One, two, three, four" together,

where on four, everyone extends any number of fingers from none to five (thumbs count as fingers here). It's critical that everyone extends their fingers simultaneously, without a lag.

The object is for the group to achieve exactly eleven extended fingers. The rub of course, is that no talking is permitted between the players at any time.

You simply move from one round of "…one, two, three, four..," extend and count the fingers (bother, sixteen), straight into the next round, and so on.

It never ceases to amaze me how often screams of delight will issue forth from a group when the magic eleven appears. Imagine if they solved something really important!

Variations

- Vary the number of people, the number of hands a person can use, and the number to be reached. For example, use two hands, permitting up to ten fingers to be extended, to achieve a sum of 23.
- Check out "Your Add" for related variations.

TRAIN STATION

A ridiculous slow-mo greeting exercise that never ends

AT A GLANCE
People move in slow motion toward one person, suddenly realise they are mistaken, and then pretend they were greeting another person.

WHAT YOU NEED
A large, open space to spread out in
Minimum of 10 greeters
5 minutes

WHAT TO DO
First up, find a fun way to divide your group into pairs (such as hop on one leg, and find another person doing the same as you). Remember your partner.

Okay, now introduce the story that your group is standing on a train station platform, waiting for their long-lost friends to arrive. They are your bestest friends in the whole-wide

world, and they have just gotten off the train. You are very excited.

Have your group spread out, explaining that partners should end up in opposite ends of the space from each other, i.e., you don't need a circle, just a semblance of distance between the two people. Instruct everyone now to imagine that you have just seen your friend get off the train, and you are each waving madly to get the other's attention. All of this occurs, however, in slow-motion. Everything, the waves, the hellos, the kisses you blow – all of the excitement – is in slow-motion.

The greetings continue, an embrace is imminent as each person gets closer and closer to the other….. until you are about a metre (a yard) away from your "friend," when you each realise – it's the wrong person! You are mortified so you immediately drop gears into dam-

age control, and pretend that you were waving to the person behind your partner all along.

Spy another person at a distance in the same predicament, start to move slowly towards them as if they are now your bestest friend in the whole-wide world, and …. the same thing happens again!

Variation

Alter the states in which people greet each other – fast-motion, sleepy-motion, drunken-motion, short-sighted (regular speed), etc.

WARM-UPS & STRETCHES

Warm-ups and stretches are those activities that provide an opportunity for group members to "get the blood moving." As a form of "de-inhibitizer," they can also set the tone for somewhat less physical but more emotionally demanding requirements of your program.

To be effective, warm-ups and stretches should feature:

- Fun as a major component
- A variety of challenges so that each person may choose their own level of physical (or emotional) involvement
- Lots of interaction among group members
- A focus on effort / trying rather than success / failure

Whole of Group Warm-ups

Freeze Frame
Fill the Space
Mission Impossible
People to People
Chic-a-boom

Partner Warm-ups

Mirror Image
Toe to Toe
Finger Fencing
Snoopy & Red Baron
Windmills
Woodcutters
Isometric Stretch (5-5-5)
Star Stretch
Skipping Rope

All of The Above

Quick Line-Up
Shipwreck
I've got the Power
Wave Stretch
Yurt Circle
Speed Rabbit
Salt & Pepper

FREEZE FRAME

A remarkably powerful warm-up of the body and mind

AT A GLANCE
A group mingles about an open space, and one by one, people freeze until the whole group has frozen.

WHAT YOU NEED
A flat, open space for mingling within boundaries
Minimum of 12 people
5 – 10 minutes

WHAT TO DO
This is so simple, yet so powerful. Have your group spread evenly throughout an open space. Ask them to wander aimlessly within the boundaries of the space, simply observing other people as they move about them. No need to talk or touch anyone. Just wander.

Explain that at any point, any one or more people can choose to "freeze" their movement, remaining absolutely dead-still mid-wander. This will trigger everyone who observes this immobilisation to immediately freeze their movements too, and so on the ripples extend.

The object for the group is to see how long it takes every individual to freeze. Hold the "group freeze" for a second or two to ensure that there are no belated moves, then….. relax.

There is no point in physically timing the attempts, because the initial freeze will be triggered at random moments every time. Repeat the task a dozen or

so times, perhaps with a few variations thrown in for good measure.

In the beginning, people are focused on little else than themselves. This exercise forces people to look beyond themselves. It's amazing what is achieved in such a short space of time, when a group of individuals constitute themselves as "community," focus on other people and agree to achieve a common goal (i.e., everybody frozen as quickly as possible). Are you starting to make connections here to your program goals?

This exercise is clearly a good physical warm-up. However, leading a brief discussion about what else is happening and how it relates to the "day-to-day" of the group may also open up some useful insights that relate to the "connectedness" of the group.

Variations

- Ask people to speed their mingling up a little, and then in a later round, add sharp, random turns in direction.
- Permit very brisk walking (shy of a jog or run) if you feel the group can keep it safe, especially with the sharp corners.

FILL THE SPACE

Perfect for large groups, promoting lots of fun and non-threatening interaction

AT A GLANCE
People mingle in a space, responding to instructions to follow, lead and evade certain other people.

WHAT YOU NEED
A large, flat open area with boundaries
Minimum of 20 people
5 – 10 minutes

WHAT TO DO
Invite your group to spread themselves randomly but evenly inside an area that you have designated. Ask each person to slowly mingle about the area and attempt to "fill the (empty) spaces" as they are created here and there. Suggest that there is no need for talking or touching, simply move and observe all that is around you.

As your group has started to mill about (notice, how funny your group will think this is already!), ask each person to secretly identify someone on the other side of the space. That other person doesn't know that you have picked them. Then, keeping that person in mind, follow as closely behind that secret person as possible – so that each time he or she moves away from you, you must follow.

Obviously (and you don't need to say this), this is a set up, because everyone is following a different person. They frantically move about to catch up with their ever-moving target. Maintaining a walking pace is important though – there's always one or two who insist on

mingling "briskly," otherwise known as running.

After a few moments, ask the group to resume their mingling, and repeat the process with a new secret admirer. Or, move on to one of the following variations.

Variations

- As you mingle, secretly identify a person close to you, and then keep as far away as possible (within the boundaries) from this person.
- Select a person on the other side again, and then try to keep an equal distance in front of them at all times. As a further twist, make sure this other person notices you!

MISSION IMPOSSIBLE

An exciting variation of Fill The Space that can be enjoyed on its own

AT A GLANCE
While mingling, a person tries to continually keep a straight line between him or herself and two other secretly-identified people. Everyone else in the group is doing the same.

WHAT YOU NEED
A large, flat open area
Minimum of 20 secret agents
5 – 10 minutes

WHAT TO DO
Similar to Fill The Space, create a space full of randomly-distributed people, and ceremonially anoint everyone as "special agents." Their mission, should they choose to accept, is to keep a close eye on a "master criminal," but they cannot under any circumstances get caught doing the spying.

The next step is for every agent to secretly identify two other people from the group (i.e., these people will not know, nor should they be told that they have been chosen) – one assumes the role of a "master criminal" in the mind of the agent, and the other will act as a "cover" concealing the agent from the criminal. Picture a straight line with the master criminal and the secret agent at opposite ends of the open space, and the cover situated somewhere between the two.

The agents' mission is to spy on the criminal, but not get caught, so they will always keep their cover situated in a straight-line, so to speak, between

themselves and the criminal. Any time the cover or the criminal moves, the agent has to move accordingly to remain concealed.

Of course, every secret agent is manoeuvring simultaneously, so it ends up just being a lot of mindless mayhem. Mission impossible, you bet!

Variations

- Ask people to identify two new secret people, this time, a "left-hand" person and a "right-hand" person. On "Go," everyone tries to keep their left-hand person, on their left-hand side at all times, while also keeping their right-hand person on ….you get the idea. A mission impossible – pretty much, it will last all of ten seconds, but a wonderful method to break down physical barriers.
- Just for fun, ask your group to freeze. Nominate one person to move their position anywhere within the area and stop. Watch what happens when you ask the rest of the group to re-position themselves. Ideal for illustrating the impact one person can have on a group!

PEOPLE TO PEOPLE

Ideal for stretching your group – anatomically speaking

AT A GLANCE
Standing in a circle, people respond to the call of a person in the middle to make contact with matching parts of their partner's body.

WHAT YOU NEED
A flat, open space for a circle
Minimum of 10 people
10 minutes

WHAT TO DO
Ask everyone in your group to find a partner and form a circle around you. To make this work, you need everyone to have a partner, except one person – you, the person starting in the middle. Pull yourself in or out of the activity to make the numbers work where necessary.

Start a beat by clapping your hands (about a clap per second) and invite everybody to join in for awhile so that they can get the hang of it. Feel free to move to the groove. It will only encourage further random acts of silliness later on. Explain that you (the person in the middle) will call out the name of any two body parts, such as "nose and elbow." On this command, everyone turns to their partner and touches their nose to their partner's elbow and vice versa. Also, keeping in time with the beat, everybody sings / calls out "nose to elbow" twice as they do it. Upon completing the anatomical shuffle, the people resume their clapping, awaiting the next command.

This routine continues several times, until the person in the middle yells "people to people" which occurs whenever they wish to change the pace, or have simply run out of anatomical ideas. At this point everybody is obligat-

ed to leave their current partner, and look for a new one. Amidst all this running about, the person in the middle works feverishly to locate a partner too. As new partners are won over, they resume the beat, and a new person (the one left without a partner) calls out the next set of body parts.

A hint, if someone calls out "lips to lips" or something to that effect in an effort to look smart or cool, keep the beat going, and respond with a smile, "Challenge by Choice."

Variations

- To provide an escape route for people who are not comfortable standing / talking in front of others, let them know that they can say "people to people" at anytime – like, as soon as they find themselves without a partner.
- Vary the rate of the beat, i.e., make it "speedy-gonzalez" or slow-motion style.

CHIC-A-BOOM!

A cool little energiser you can dance and sing to!

AT A GLANCE
A group song and dance that invites people to gradually groove into the centre of the circle.

WHAT YOU NEED
A flat, open space to accommodate a moving, grooving circle
Minimum of 12 groovers
5 – 10 minutes.

WHAT TO DO
Stand with your group as part of a circle, and teach them these groovy moves.

With index fingers, point up into the sky alternating thrusts of each hand to a beat, i.e., left-hand up, then right-hand up, etc. Now, something similar, but point down with alternate thrusts towards the ground.

Next, point your fingers to the left in and out, in and out, as you take little rocking steps to the left. And finally, point your fingers to the right, in and out, in and out as you're taking jaunty little rocking steps to the right.

Okay, as you can tell, it's all in the delivery, but you've got the moves. Here's the tune.

"Hey there (enter name), you're a real cool cat.

You've gotta lot of this, and you've gotta lot of that.

So come on in and get down......

....aaaand, up chic-a-boom, chic-a-boom, chic-a-boom.

And down chic-a-boom, chic-a-boom, chic-a-boom.

To the left, chic-a-boom, chic-a-boom, chic-a-boom.

To the right, chic-a-boom, chic-a-boom, chic-a-boom. "

Now it's time to put it all together. It starts with one person in the centre (you perhaps?) who will sing the first part of the little ditty, with attitude just dripping off you. Sing as you look directly at someone, use their name as indicated, and when you get to the "come on in and get down…" part, you side up to this person, take them in your arm and lead them into the central limelight of the circle. Then, you, your new cool cat, and everyone still standing in the circle thinking "when am I going to be dragged in?" will launch into a medley of "chic-a-booms" replete with groovy moves and spunk. The up, down, left and right pointing of hands accompanies the chic-a-booms beat-box style.

Once you have sung the verse through, every person in the centre (it doubles with every verse) will turn to another standing in the circle and start all over again. Two begets four, four begets eight, and within four or five verses, you've got everyone in the circle having a great time. And might I say, looking very cooool.

Variation

Oh no, Chic-a-boom is way too cool for variations, but I guess you could be permitted to alter some of the lyrics or dance moves!

MIRROR IMAGE

Excellent for stimulating mutual cooperation and plenty of unself-conscious stretching

AT A GLANCE
Facing each other, one person will reproduce the "mirror image" of the moves of his or her partner.

WHAT YOU NEED
A flat, open space
Minimum of 2 people
5 minutes

WHAT TO DO
Ask people to find a partner who is about their height, and gather around. Start with a demonstration, inviting a volunteer to face you standing about half a metre apart. You initiate the action while the other person becomes your "mirror image." Get that, it's a mirror image, so if I extend my left arm out to my left-side, my partner will extend their right arm out to their right-side.

The intention is to make your movements interesting and slow enough for the other person to mime as if he or she were a full-length mirror. The enjoyment level is definitely enhanced by an initial zany presentation of unself-conscious stretching. Try not to succumb to typical "star jump" types of stretches. Rather, for example, invent an innovative and fun morning "wake up" routine that includes having a shower, dressing in stretchy trousers and a long-sleeve angora sweater, etc.

It's now time to turn it over to the group. The facial and physical gymnastics that result let you see people as you've never seen them before. Swap roles after an appropriate time.

TOE TO TOE

A gentle slow-motion "push me-pull me" stretch

AT A GLANCE
Two people face each other in a shaking-hands position standing one foot behind the other on a line, moving slowly to pull the other person off balance.

WHAT YOU NEED
A flat, open space
Minimum of 2 people
5 minutes

WHAT TO DO
Ask your group to split up into pairs. Invite a volunteer forward, and position yourselves so that you are facing each other as if standing on a thin line. That is, the toes of your right shoes point toward the other person on the line, and your left foot is directly behind the heels of your right shoe. If you're finding it difficult to keep your balance at this point, then you've got it right!

Move close enough to your partner, so that your right toes are touching, and using your right hands, engage in a hand-shake. You're all set. The object for each person is using the movement of any part of your body, except your feet, to bring your partner off-balance. At all times, you must keep your feet on the imaginary line, and your hands clasped.

Notice I did not say "push them" or "shove them." Indeed, all movements must be made in slow-motion. There can be no sharp, thrusting movements, or any other contact made with the other to cause a sudden shift of weight. Often, as one person feels that they are about to lose their balance, they effectively bring their partner with them because they are still connected via their sweaty hands. Happily, two hands-together and four feet on the ground is usually enough to prevent a fall.

Variations

- Same exercise in reverse, with left toes forward, and left hands clasped.
- Try it with varying distances between the toes "on the line."

FINGER FENCING

Try this out for some swash-buckling fun and interaction

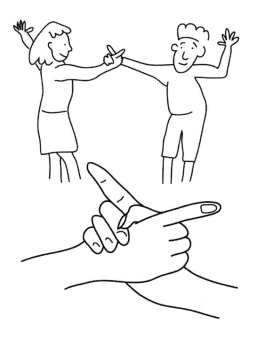

AT A GLANCE
Two people, connected by their right hands with their index fingers extended, attempt to be the first to tag the other below the waist.

WHAT YOU NEED
A flat, open space to accommodate lots of frenetic activity
Minimum of 2 swash-bucklers
5 minutes.

WHAT TO DO
Ask everyone to find a suitable "Errol Flynn" partner and a space to engage in a grand duel. Invite one promising "swash-buckler" to step forward to help you demonstrate this exercise.

This is where your zany over-the-top impression of Errol Flynn will impress everyone to give it a go. First, you need to dress for the part, so slip into your fencing suit, put on your mask, and "swish-swish" your foil. Bow to your partner, and then extend both of your right hands forward to join in one of those funky handshakes, you know, those cool clasp-your-partner's-thumb-on-top handshakes. From this position, you each extend your index finger out as if you were pointing down the fore-arm of your partner. Announce with flourish that this finger is ....your foil.

Place your other hand elegantly in the air behind you sixteenth-century style, turn side-on and lift the toe of your front foot, and voila – you're ready to engage in "mortal combat."

With a call of "On guard!" the match begins. Feet shuffle and foils swish everywhere. The first person to touch the other with their finger (foil) somewhere on the body below their waist (and beyond their wrist), exclaims "Touché" and is declared the winner.

Variation

Try using your left arm to create the foil.

SNOOPY & THE RED BARON

A playful re-creation of the popular "Peanuts" cartoon strip

AT A GLANCE
Two people facing each other, feet fixed in place, use one hand each in an attempt to make contact with the other person's hand.

WHAT YOU NEED
An open space
Minimum of 2 people
2 minutes

WHAT TO DO
Find a partner who shares a favourite "Peanuts" cartoon character with you. As you may have guessed, more than a modicum of imagination will be required for this activity.

Stand facing your partner, about a half-metre (about 20 inches) away with your feet spread about shoulder-width

apart. Each of you can use only one hand. It doesn't matter which one. Choose who wants to be Snoopy and who wants to be the evil Red Baron, and then accept that the life-like fleshy thing at the end of your arm is your chosen character. Tuck Snoopy and the Red Baron safely away into your pockets, also referred to as the aircraft hangars.

Snoopy and the Red Baron are cleared for take off on the word "Go" and each person pulls out their character and starts to flail their arms about valiantly in an effort to make contact with the enemy aircraft, i.e., your partner's hand. All movement is permitted, except that you cannot move your feet, and you cannot make contact with any other part of the "aircraft carrier." As soon as one person makes contact with the other person's hand, the aircraft is deemed to have been shot out of the air, and you can move onto the next round. Or, swap characters.

Variation

Bring out the reinforcements – each person is entitled to use both hands, giving each of them twice the chance of air-borne success.

WINDMILLS

An excellent lower-back stretch that looks worse than it really is

AT A GLANCE
Standing back to back, two people apply pressure against their outstretched arms, and wave them about gently in an arc over their heads while remaining connected.

WHAT YOU NEED
A flat, open space
Minimum of 2 people
5 minutes

WHAT TO DO
This is another one of those "look-at-the-picture-to-get-the-idea" type of activities. Start by separating your group into partners of similar heights. Standing back to back, each person will extend their arms out to their sides, and cross arms slightly to apply pressure against each other's hands. You'll look a bit like a human cross now. Suggest to people that they do not hold hands (as is their tendency) to allow ample opportunities for choice later on.

First of all, start a gentle rocking motion with your arms, as if the co-joined arms were the blades of a windmill. Up and down, up and down, this feels so good. Soon enough, you will be ready to bring one set of arms over the tops of your heads, so that each person's elbows pass in front of his or her nose. Continue to apply pressure to the hands (and this is why we don't hold them), as the arms now fold over to the other side of the body from whence

they grew. At this point, if both partners are comfortable, they may go one step further, and direct these arms down toward the ground (crossing in front of your chest) and then poke the other arms up and through the gap created by the contorted arms. Like I said, check out the illustration.

From here, untangle the arms by reversing gears, and repeat the process with the other arms on the other side. It's important to take it slowly, and then as you develop a little dexterity, you can honestly produce enough speed and therefore wind to power a mill!

Variation

Windmills went out of fashion many years ago, so we just have one version.

WOODCUTTERS

Perfect one-minute warm-up for those cold winter days

AT A GLANCE
Two people face each other holding each other's hands in a "monkey grip" and push and pull their arms back and forth toward each other, slowly gathering speed.

WHAT YOU NEED
A flat, open space
Minimum of 2 lumberjacks or jills
1 minute

WHAT TO DO
Everyone needs a partner. Facing each other, ask them to hold hands in what's known as the "monkey's grip" position, where the fingers of each person curl inside the palm of their partner, and the thumbs sit on top.

Look each other squarely in the eye, and slowly – and I mean slowly – start pumping away with your arms. Push your left arm out, while pulling your right arm in, back and forth, back and forth. Like a steam train that is gathering momentum chug by chug, you get faster and faster, until you think you can't go any faster. But you try, and you do go faster, and finally – pfffttt – you fall down in a heap on the ground and can't believe you were feeling cold a moment ago!

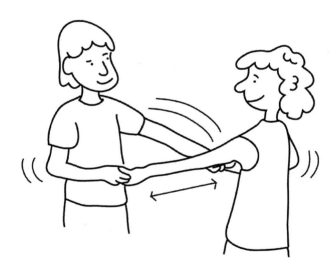

Variation
Form a tight circle of fellow lumberjacks or jills, and hold the hands of your two neighbours. You know the rest.

ISOMETRIC STRETCH (5-5-5)

They say isometric is the best form of exercise – give it a go!

AT A GLANCE
Partners invent creative methods to apply, hold and release isometric pressure against different parts of their bodies in 5 second intervals.

WHAT YOU NEED
A flat, open space where it is possible to lie down
Minimum of 2 people
10 minutes

WHAT TO DO
I'm running out of ways to write "find a partner," so how about I just turn around, and you'll magically find someone next to you by the time I turn around.

With a partner, move off to a comfortable area for a few minutes and discover as many different ways two people can apply pressure to their bodies using one another – no props, no other weight, just the two of you. The trick is, once you have established the position, to build the pressure for five seconds (without forcing the other person off balance), to hold that peak of pressure for five seconds, and then release the pressure gradually for the final five seconds.

This is what it could look like. Two people choose to stand facing each other, and place their right hands against each other. As the five seconds tick away, it will seem as if the hands are not moving – even though considerable pressure is being applied (i.e., that's what isometrics is all about).

Scratching for ideas of what partners could do here? Think about the options available to two people when they are standing facing one another, leaning in to one another, side by side, back to back, lying on the ground next to, and end to end of each other. How's that for starters?

Variations

- Upon bunching everyone up at the end, invite one or more partners to demonstrate an isometric stretch they discovered, and ask everyone to try it.
- Try groups of three or four people.

STAR STRETCH

Superb partner stretch that takes on star proportions

AT A GLANCE
Two people work together to create a counter-weighted star formation with their bodies.

WHAT YOU NEED
A flat, open space with a non-slip surface if possible
Minimum of 2 stars
15 – 20 minutes

WHAT TO DO
This is one of those activities that benefits from (a) watching two people demonstrate what it looks like first, and (b) building up your group's skills slowly. I'm going to take you through several levels.

Start by facing your partner, feet together and holding each other's wrists (this tends to be the strongest form of link for high performance star-stretchers). With a gap of approximately 30cm (12 inches) from the end of your feet to your partner's, each person will lean back slowly trying hard not to bend their body, i.e., they pivot from their ankles. From the side, it will look like the letter A sitting upside-down on its pointy end. The idea is to be able to lean back and feel as if the angle and weight of your partner is supporting you completely, and you could stay like this forever. For some couples, particularly if there is a large weight difference, this will take some time to perfect.

To ramp up the challenge, encourage each person to bring their feet closer to their partner's, and eventually "overtake" them so that in effect, their feet pass to the side, and possibly even behind their partner's feet. Oooooweee!

Next step, each person stands with

their back to their partner, and reverses the first stretch, i.e., extend behind and grab the arms of the other person, with bodies leaning forward this time. Making a firm and comfortable grip at the start is the hardest part of this step of the exercise, but totally doable. Again, it's a great challenge to have your feet pass your partners, and remain balanced.

Now, having progressed so far, here is the ultimate challenge. Standing side by side, with the two inside-feet right up against each other, each person only grasps the inside arm of their partner. By leaning away from their partner, each person will attempt to lift their outside leg off the ground, remain balanced and then shift their airborne foot toward their partner. Their aim is to touch the soles of their feet / shoes together, throw their outside arms up into the air and shout "Hey, look at this everyone!"

Variation

Actually, I lied, this is the ultimate challenge – same as above, but each person faces the opposite direction from their partner, perform the star stretch as above, but this time their soles touch inside the gap formed between the two inside legs. I love this activity.

SKIPPING ROPE

A skipping rope exercise you'll never trip up on

AT A GLANCE
Individuals and partners skip an imaginary rope and play tricks with each other.

WHAT YOU NEED
A flat, open space with ample space to spread out
Minimum of 10 people
5 minutes

WHAT TO DO
Ever tripped up on a skipping rope? This one's for you.

Spread your group out, way out, and ask everyone to bend down and pick up their very own skipping rope. When they observe you do this and pick up what appears to be nothing, yet shake it out as if you really were holding a rope in front, they'll soon get the idea.

Start off slowly by turning the (imaginary) rope over your body a few times. Once you have warmed up and become accustomed to the pace and responsive qualities of your rope, try these illusions on for size:

- Skip rope as fast as you can as you move about the area.

- Spin your rope as many times as possible in one jump. Shout out your record.

- Cross the rope in front of you as you jump, i.e., "Double Dutch."

- Spin your rope backwards.
- Skip up to another person and introduce them into your rope, skipping

in time together, and vice versa. Start by facing one another, then go back to back.

Variation

Okay, one more. Skip up to another person, and toss your rope to them mid-skip as they toss theirs to you. Trick is to keep your partner's rope spinning as you catch it.

QUICK LINE-UP

Fast-paced action warm-up that never fails to raise a smile and a sweat

AT A GLANCE
Teams of people move quickly to return to their pre-determined positions relative to the person standing in the middle.

WHAT YOU NEED
A large, flat open space
Minimum of 8 people
5 – 10 minutes

WHAT TO DO
Divide your group into four teams of roughly even numbers. Stand in the middle of a square which is formed by the members of each team standing next to each other on one side of the square. To reinforce who is on what team, ask the members of each side of the square to hold hands (i.e., the corner people don't hold), and when you point to their team, they all raise their

arms high in the air, and scream, "Quick Line-Up!". Bonus points for whoever is the loudest.

Deliberately face one of the teams. Nominate this team as "north" and the team behind you as "south," on your left is "west" and on your right is "east." Pretty simple. Yet, when you shift position, say a full 90 degrees to your right, you are now directly facing the "east" team. Then, explain that as soon as you say, "Quick Line Up" (which is like saying, "Go"), every team has to release their hands, and move as quickly as possible back into their original positions relative to you, i.e., north will always end up facing you, south will always be behind you, etc, etc.

The first team to return to their original positions, raise their coupled hands and shout, "Quick Line Up" wins. Have fun teasing people, and move outside the initial boundaries of the square. Make sure that no one moves an inch, until you say, "Quick Line Up". And for safety purposes, ensure that people release their hands before they move to re-position themselves.

Variations

- Just for fun, lie down facing up, down or on your side and see what happens (but be prepared for "stacks on the mill").
- Give a triangle or a polygon a try.

SHIPWRECK

Classic energiser that involves listening and rapid response skills

AT A GLANCE
Individuals and small groups respond as quickly as possible to the "captain's" instructions to perform a series of tasks on board an imaginary ship.

WHAT YOU NEED
A large, flat and open space with boundaries
Minimum of 15 sailors
15 – 20 minutes

WHAT TO DO
With everyone gathered around, teach your group a series of sea-worthy chores to perform on your imaginary tall ship's deck. First of all, point out where or along which boundaries the bow (front), stern (rear), port (left) and starboard (right) sides of the ship can be located.

Next, describe the appropriate actions for the following commands.

"Attention" – individuals stand to attention, saluting with their right hand.

"Swab the Deck" – individuals get on their hands and knees and scrub the deck.

"Sailor Overboard" – everyone drops to the floor on either the port or starboard edges of the deck.

"Lifeboats" – three people form a single file line, sit down and pretend to row a boat.

"Rig the Sails" – two people join hands and pretend to be setting up the sails.

The game starts with everyone standing on the deck, i.e., centre of the space. The captain will then issue a series of commands, including instructions to send everyone to the "bow," "stern," "port" and "starboard" sides of the deck.

You need to understand that the captain is a masochist, because he or she loves to send people to the bow, then the stern, to rig the sails, then back to the bow, to the port, to swab the deck, all within 30 seconds. And he's just warming up. It's high energy, suspenseful fun, with no particular ending. Unless of course, you take on a popular variation.

Variations

Introduce an elimination element. Sailors can be eliminated when:

- A sailor is the last to perform a particular chore, or get to the designated side of the deck.
- A sailor is the "odd one out" when chores require two or three sailors to complete.
- The captain calls, "Attention." He or she must say, "At ease" before anyone can perform any other chores, i.e., a sailor is eliminated (lost at sea) when they respond (move) to a trick command;
- The captain calls, "Sailor Overboard" – everyone who is still on deck, may rescue a sailor who has been "lost at sea," i.e., those who have been eliminated (this keeps the action going).

I'VE GOT THE POWER

A design-your-own-stretch activity

AT A GLANCE
People take turns demonstrating quirky stretches that their group is obliged to imitate.

WHAT YOU NEED
A flat, open space to accommodate a circle
Minimum of 8 people
5 – 10 minutes

WHAT TO DO
It is not necessary to create a circle for this exercise, but it's useful, because half the fun is discovered in the looks of delight and torment as people try out some unusual stretches.

Pull an imaginary "sphere of power" out of your pocket to kick off the activity. Explain to your group that this "power" has the ability to enable them to do whatever the person holding it chooses to do. For example…this is where I exhibit some silly stretch that would never be seen in your common garden-variety PE text-book. You then invite everyone else to join in the action.

Relish the power for about 15 to 20 seconds, and then select another person on the other side of the circle, and toss the "sphere" over to them, perhaps calling their name first. Joke around, and enroll them in the whimsy of your pass, and ensure that they catch it. If they don't, perhaps pick it up off the ground, and hand it to them – they'll get the idea. It's now their turn to transform the group, and so on it goes. They can choose to do whatever they want, but try to crank up the "weird and wonderful." With encouragement, you may avoid the horror of falling into the same-old same-old world of "star-jumps," "push-ups" and "tummy crunches."

Variation

Same set-up, with a "micro-macro" twist. One person starts with a really small, barely noticeable movement (e.g., blinking their eyes several times), then throws the power to the next person who is obliged to take on a really large-make-you-sweat movement (e.g., jogging on the spot raising knees as high as you can). Then back to a micro movement again, and so on.

WAVE STRETCH

A design-you-own-stretch activity that will linger longer

AT A GLANCE
A fun stretch is introduced by one person and is quickly assumed by everyone else one by one – in a wave-like motion around the circle.

WHAT YOU NEED
A flat, open space to accommodate a large circle
Minimum of 8 wavers
5 -10 minutes

WHAT TO DO
Set yourself up as part of a circle, with plenty of room between each person. Start off by demonstrating a fun little exercise that everyone can perform, e.g., waving your arms out by your side up and down like angel wings. Immediately the person to your left is asked to imitate your actions, and then the next person to their left, and so on. The movement is passed around the circle much like "the wave," you know that ubiquitous "raising up of arms one after another" motion that swept every major sporting arena during the 1990s.

Unlike what happens in today's sporting stadiums, everyone in the circle keeps doing the movement (even after the wave has passed them by), until.....the wave returns to the person who introduced the movement to the group. Now, the wave passes this person by, and the person to their left introduces a new movement, e.g., hopping on one leg whistling Dixie. Get this, the first person who introduces the angel wings keeps flapping until the wave of hopping comes around to him /

her. That is to say, whoever introduces a movement will perform it for two complete rotations of the circle.

In essence, everyone keeps doing whatever they are doing, until the person to their right is struck by the wave and takes on the new movement. A hint – think carefully about what you're going to subject your group to, because you'll end up doing it twice as long.

Variation

Send a "wave" of two movements / stretches at the same time, but in different directions. There will be total chaos, but tons of fun.

YURT CIRCLE

An extraordinary cooperative group activity that is self-supporting

AT A GLANCE
Holding hands firmly in a circle, people lean out as far as they feel comfortable, being supported by the rest of the group.

WHAT YOU NEED
A flat, open space with a non-slip surface if possible

Minimum of 10 yurts
5 – 10 minutes

WHAT TO DO
Ask your group to form a perfect circle, and then firmly grasp the hands or wrists of their neighbours. A good, strong, yet comfortable grip is essential, because you may apply pressure to it

for a minute or more. Stretch the circle out, not quite to its limits, but certainly, all arms should be extended.

Now, with feet placed together and securely planted on the ground, instruct everyone to slowly and gently lean backwards. Suggest that it may be necessary to adjust the position of some people's feet so that every person can support the weight not only of their immediate neighbours, but that generated by the whole group. A group will rarely "get this" off the bat, but persevere, it may take a few goes (and a few collapses!) before the group succeeds.

The ultimate is for most if not all the people of your group to experience a feeling of total support, i.e., as if they could "park" in this position all day without effort. No matter the size, shape or abilities of your group, this "yurt" or self supporting structure is totally possible. It just takes a little cooperation and an acceptance that everyone is different.

Variation

With an even number of people, ask that every second person leans in on "go" while every other person leans out of the circle as above. Once equilibrium is reached, ask that the positions are swapped, but for a challenge, have them try to move into this alternate position from where they are now.

SPEED RABBIT

A classic cooperative "do-this-quickly-or-you're-out" activity

AT A GLANCE
At the behest of a person pointing from the middle of a circle, groups of three people work together to create a specific "animal" with their bodies as quickly as possible.

WHAT YOU NEED
A flat, open space
Minimum of 10 people
10 – 15 minutes

WHAT TO DO
Ask your group to form one line in which every person has a neighbour on both sides of them. Of course, it just so happens the two ends of this line must meet. Ah, a circle!

First up, establish the creation of three animals – let's say, an elephant, a cow and a kangaroo. Calling on the creative talents of your group, explain that each animal needs the assistance of three people to come into being, i.e., one middle person and two neighbours. Your group can help you develop the anatomy, but here's a glimpse of what might transpire:

Elephant: One person uses their arms to create the elephant's trunk, while the other two create huge flappy ears with their arms.

Cow: One person interlocks their fingers, turns this structure up-side down and points their thumbs to the

ground, while the other two grab a thumb each and start milking, as if it was the cow's udder.

Kangaroo: One person forms a pouch with their arms in front of them, while the other two make contact with the first person's shoulders and thump their feet on the ground to become the kangaroo's powerful legs.

With these images in mind, explain that the person in the middle – the "pointer" – will aim at any one person in the circle and call out the name of one of the three animals. Immediately, this person and his or her two neighbours will spring into action and create the desired and anatomically correct animal. The "pointer" person will count to ten as fast as possible, suggesting that if the animal is not created either correctly, or by the time he / she gets to "ten," the most deserving of the other three will be invited to swap positions with the pointer, and the game starts anew.

Naturally, as the groups start to settle into this routine, unsettle them by adding one or more pointers into the centre to keep up the energy and sheer cacophony of the moment.

Variations

- Introduce a fourth or even fifth animal. Make them distinctly different, i.e., even if every animal has to have ears, make sure they are not similar to each other.
- Experiment with other forms, such as occupations, famous people, sports or corporate attributes.
- Combine this exercise with the likes of Zip Zap and Bumpity Bump Bump Bump.

SALT & PEPPER

A classic warm-up that is as timeless as it is absorbing.

AT A GLANCE
Standing with their group, individuals attempt to jump to the desired side of a line immediately upon the instruction of the "leader."

WHAT YOU NEED
A flat, open space with a long line marked on the ground
Minimum of 8 people
10 – 15 minutes

WHAT TO DO
Ask your group to stand directly to one side of a line marked on the ground; for example, a basketball court boundary. From your perspective, the group will appear spread out in a single file formation within a few inches of the line. Identify two clearly distinct areas that will represent the two sides of the line, e.g., one side is the "salt" and the other is the "pepper." It may just as well be "pool" and "bleachers" or "field" and "building" representing the geography of the area you are playing within. It totally doesn't matter, as long as the areas are clear.

It's pretty simple from here. You call out, "Salt" or "Pepper" and the group, one by one but at the same time, must jump to or remain on the side which represents the call. It could sound something like this "....Salt.....Pepper....

Salt....Salt...". When you are completely unpredictable – both in terms of pace and timing – the suspense is palpable. A little teasing doesn't go astray either, such as "...Ssssssspepper...".

Here's the rub. If someone jumps when they shouldn't, or is too slow in their jumping, or – if you want to be completely ruthless – a person flinches slightly as if they were going to jump, these folks are "out of the game." Now, you get to decide what that means of course. Typically, those who make an error must leave the group, and the game will continue to determine a "winner." In these circumstances, I suggest inviting one of the "eliminated" to make the next calls.

Variation
Give everyone three "lives" before they have to say bye-bye.

TAG GAMES

Although primarily fun, tag activities are useful as warm-up exercises wherein group members are able to take some "risks," e.g., exert energy, run around like a fool, and touch others in a safe environment.

Tag type activities should feature:

- Fun as a major component
- A safe framework in which each person may choose their own level of physical (or emotional) involvement
- Lots of interaction among group members
- A focus on participation rather than win / lose

Partner Tags

Toe Tag
Triangle Tag
Knee Slap
Hip Tag

Whole of Group Tags

Elbow Tag
Walk (Pairs) Tag
Blob Tag
Heads & Tails Tag
Just Like Me Tag
Hug Tag
Lemonade
Giants Elves Wizards
Everybody's It
Hospital Tag
Dead Ant Tag
Basketball Court Tag
Name Tag

TOE TAG

A hop-step-and-jump tag game that quickly raises the energy of your group

AT A GLANCE
Starting back to back, two partners spin around on "Go" and try to "tag" the toe of their partner before they get tagged.

WHAT YOU NEED
A flat, open space to accommodate lots of frenetic activity
Minimum of 2 toe-taggers
2 – 5 minutes

WHAT TO DO
This is a perfect two-minute filler that has the power to transform your mopey group into a ball of energy.

You need groups made up of partners. Ask everyone to start with their backs to their partner, and on an appropriate signal like "Go," both partners spin around 180 degrees to face one another and engage in a dance-like combat. Each person attempts to "tag" the toe of their partner gently before one of their own feet gets tagged.

Be sure to remind your group that you said "tagged" and not "stomped." This will make all the difference between many fun rounds, and a lot of sore feet. Play best of three rounds, but if you lose the first two, better make it five!

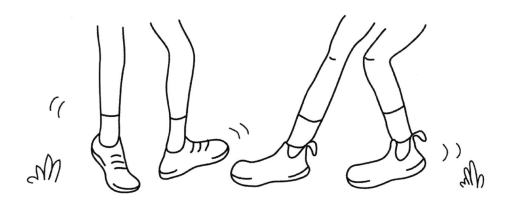

Variations
- If too much energy is expended chasing your partner, a less aerobic version is to start by facing your partner and holding his or her hands.
- Form a circle with your group holding hands. Each person attempts to "tag" the feet of their immediate neighbours. As soon as a person has had both feet tagged, they retreat from the circle. The group re-joins, and the game continues until the final two "toe taggers" duel.

TRIANGLE TAG

High energy leave 'em panting tag game.

AT A GLANCE
Three people hold hands to form a triangle, and move quickly to prevent a fourth person on the outside from making a tag.

WHAT YOU NEED
A flat, open space for lots of frenetic action
Minimum of 4 taggers
5 minutes

WHAT TO DO
Choose a random method to divide your assembly into groups of four people. Ask three of the people to form a triangle within the circle by holding hands facing each other. Identify which one of the three people in the triangle is designated to be tagged and which two are the protectors of that person.

The fourth person is the tagger, and his or her job is to move around the outside of the triangle and tag the "tagee." This is a tough gig – within 15 seconds of high-energy pursuit, I guarantee that most taggers will be ready to quit. I suggest that if a tag is not achieved within 30 seconds, or the tagger collapses beforehand, a new tagger is identified, and these two people swap roles.

Note – some die-hard taggers will want to reach across the circle, or dive under the arms of the triangle to mark their prey, but these are all no-go zones.

Variations
- The triangle is formed by holding onto shoulders rather than hands, i.e., makes it slightly easier for the tagger.
- Use four people to form the, um… triangle.

KNEE SLAP

Great energiser as much as a tag game

AT A GLANCE
Two people facing each other, with hands placed on their knees, try to tag one or both knees of their partner when the latter's hands are lifted.

WHAT YOU NEED
A flat, open space
Minimum of 2 slappers
2 minutes

WHAT TO DO
Ask everyone to find a partner who has knees that look like theirs. Of course, this is a completely frivolous request, because all you really need is lots of pairs, but observing the brief pursuit of knee comparison is worth it.

Standing with their feet about shoulder-width apart, each person faces their partner about a metre (40 inches) away and bends down slightly to place their hands on their knees. Each combatant eyes the other eagerly and the action begins. A score is made when one person tags the free-knee of the other, i.e., their partner does not have a hand on that knee for a split second. Naturally, in order to make a tag, a person's hand must vacate their knee, so they are vulnerable to attack as well.

Mr or Ms Smarty-pants will think that

if they never take their hands off their knees they can't lose. Perhaps, but what a boring way to live your life – which is what we're talking about here, right?

Safety note – watch your head. The focus is all about the knees and hands, thus a tendency to forget about the possibility of bumping heads as people dart about to prevent being tagged.

Variations

- Same deal, but once play has started, no one can move their feet.
- Form a group of three or four people. Same game, but now you have many more knees to slap. Once a person "loses" both knees, they remove themselves from the action, and the circle re-joins.

HIP TAG

An excellent "win-win" activity that combines learning and fun

AT A GLANCE
Two people, standing side-by-side, clasp hands and try to have the back of their partner's hand touch their hip as many times as possible.

WHAT YOU NEED
An open space
Minimum of 2 people
2 minutes

WHAT TO DO
Ask your group to form pairs, standing side by side with their partners, holding hands. Now take note of how people orient their hands. Stereotypically speaking, boys tend to prefer to face their palm backwards, (the "taking" position), while women tend to prefer the "giving" position with their palm facing forwards. Doesn't mean anything, just interesting when two people hold hands and discover that they both prefer to orient their hands the same way. But hey, you've got the group laughing already.

Instruct each pair that they are about to engage in a quick activity in which, as individuals, their mission is to cause the back of their partner's hand (that part which is closest to your hip) to touch their own hip as often as is possible. Naturally, your partner is trying to do the same thing with the back of your hand against their hip. Okay, not much else required – go!

Let it run for say 10 -15 seconds, no more. What I expect you'll see is one of two outcomes. One, typically the most common, will reflect a tense, almost feverish hive of activity as each person "competes" valiantly to force the back of their partner's hand to touch their hip. This is good, and if you

have been careful in your briefing, will create lots of energy conducive to a fun time. The second outcome, which often emerges (but not always) as if it was supposed to happen this way anyway, will uncover relatively sedate looking partners simply moving their clasped hands back and forth, back and forth as fast as they can between their respective hips.

So, who is right? What happened? First, I would suggest you quickly do the rounds of the group, asking for each partnership to report back to the group on their aggregate score (pick the really competitive ones first). Scores such as one, two, or maybe three are not uncommon. Then ask one of the more demure partners for their score – it will probably be something like 40, or 50, or something so large, you can almost hear the jaws of the competitive folks hit the ground. You are now ready for a quick lesson.

The difference illustrates how quickly we can view a given situation with a "win – lose" mentality, yet with just a little bit of collaboration, can turn into a positive "win – win" outcome. If you go back now and re-read my instructions above, you'll find that I never did say that you had to get more than your partner. But the simple pitting of one person against another is a sure fire way to reach a competitive outcome. That's okay, this activity is a wonderful catalyst for discussing "win – win" scenarios. Or, if nothing else, have fun.

Variation

Deliver the activity to two (physically separate) groups. The first group is instructed as above, while the second group (who did not hear or see the first group engage) is given perhaps a more collaborative briefing. Excellent opportunity to reflect on the difference our language can make.

ELBOW TAG

One of the best adaptations of tiggy I know

AT A GLANCE
One person chases another around a group of partners who have linked arms, waiting for either the "tagger" or "tagee" to link up with one of the linked partners to immediately create a new cat or mouse.

WHAT YOU NEED
A large, flat open space
Minimum of 10 pairs of elbows
10 minutes

WHAT TO DO
Ask each person to find a partner, and link arms / elbows with them. Their outside arms should be positioned like a tea-cup handle (with hand on hip). If you have an uneven number of people, create one trio. Each pair is then encouraged to find their own space (within specified boundaries) so that they are not too close to the other pairs, i.e., you don't need a circle formation.

Two people volunteer to become a cat – the "tagger" – and a mouse – the "tagee." On "Go," the cat chases the mouse in an effort to tag him or her somewhere below the shoulders (notice the word "tag" is used and not "tackle"). The chase occurs in and around the other pairs, who are fixed in their positions, until they get tagged, or the mouse chooses to link with any one of the linked pairs' outside arms.

If the mouse chooses to link, it's a case of "two's company, three's a crowd." So the partner with whom the mouse did not directly link, will release their arm from their partner, enter the fray and become the new "mouse," i.e., the old mouse swaps roles with him or her. The cat resumes the chase. If and when a tag is made, the cat and mouse reverse roles.

As your group appears to grasp this tagging concept, introduce a second (and third....) "cat" and "mouse" for increased action and fun. Any cat can chase any mouse. Stand back for mondo confusion, laughter and plenty of spontaneous, uninhibited fun.

Variations

- As above, but allow the cat to also seek shelter with a linked-pair, and in so doing create a new cat.
- To avoid a terminally long reign as a cat (or mouse), introduce the rule that if a tag or link is not made within ten seconds, the roles of the cat and mouse automatically reverse.

WALK (PAIRS) TAG

A simple tag that's perfect for a small area

AT A GLANCE
Participants chase their partners in a restricted area in which every other person is engaged in a similar chase.

WHAT YOU NEED
A flat, open space with boundaries
Minimum of 10 walkers
5 – 10 minutes

WHAT TO DO
Invite everyone to enter the boundaries of a restricted area, say 5m x 5m (16.5 ft x 16.5 ft.) for a group of 15 – 20 people with their partners. Request that each partnership works out quickly who is going to be "It," for example, the first person to say, "I'm not 'It'…" won't be.

The object of this tag is for each tagger to tag their partner, who, of course, is working feverishly to keep from being tagged. If a tag is made, they switch roles at which point the new "tagger" must spin 720 degrees around on the spot to allow time for the new "tagee" to escape.

Taken as is, this could be a very boring game. Except for one very important element – every other pair is playing the same game in the same area at the same time. Naturally, for safety's sake, a couple of rules apply. One, only walking is allowed (no running), and two, everyone must avoid touching anybody else in the pursuit of, or escape from, their partner.

As the game proceeds, and tags get harder to come by, most people do come into contact with others. That's expected. For this reason, it's a good idea to instruct your group at the start to assume the "bumpers up" position.

This will require everybody to place their hands in front of their chest, palms facing forward, pointing their elbows toward their bodies. Everyone keeps this "I'm ready" position through-out the game. For a bit of fun, ask people to issue an appropriate warning such as "Don't touch me" when it appears likely that someone is about to collide with them and cause contact!

Variations

- Exactly the same as above, except everyone joins physically with a partner – by way of hands or linked arms – and chases another coupled-pair. Note: partners may only travel around others, and not under or over people's arms.
- Make the boundaries very close, but still permitting movement and drop the rule regarding "no contact with any other person." If a level of safety consciousness has been developed in the earlier versions, you will note that fewer "safety issues" will arise despite the close quarters.

BLOB TAG

An ideal tag for introducing a little strategy and cooperation

AT A GLANCE
Two linked participants pursue other co-joined partners in an effort to make a tag and have the latter join the ends of their ever-expanding blob of taggers.

WHAT YOU NEED
A very large, flat open space with boundaries
Minimum of 10 taggers
10 – 15 minutes

WHAT TO DO
Separate everyone into pairs according to roughly similar physical abilities. It's not critical, just nice. Ask for one pair to volunteer as the initial "blob" or taggers. They will be "It" for the entire game, and must maintain a physical link with each other at all times as they pursue other co-joined couples.

As soon as the blob makes a (compassionate) tag, the newly-tagged pair will separate and rejoin on either side of the initial taggers, i.e., once there were two, now there are four. The blob just got a little harder to escape.

The chase continues until everyone is caught, with just a few caveats. If at any time the taggers should break links anywhere within the blob, whoever they are chasing, or perhaps just tagged, is released back into the wild. Vice versa, if while being chased a couple should lose their grip on one another, they are automatically blobbed. No matter how long the blob becomes, only the two people at the ends can make a tag.

Also, despite the attraction of running through the middle of a very wide blob to escape the evil clutches of the end taggers, all action must naturally occur around the outside and not under or over the blob's linked arms.

HEADS & TAILS TAG

A fast-paced tag in which you are both the chaser and the chased

AT A GLANCE
On "Go," participants declare their allegiance to one of two teams. The chase resumes until everyone on the opposing team is tagged.

WHAT YOU NEED
A large, flat open space with boundaries if possible
Minimum of 10 taggers
5 – 10 minutes

WHAT TO DO
Instruct participants to spread themselves randomly about the playing field / space. Explain that there are two "teams" – heads and tails – and everybody gets to choose which team they (initially) want to be on. To be on the "heads" team, a participant must place both of their hands on top of their head, while everyone belonging to the "tails" team will place their hands on their bottoms.

From the centre of the field, you announce that you will count to three quickly, at which point everyone must have demonstrated an affiliation with either the "heads" or "tails" team. On three, the chase begins. Heads chase tails, and tails chase heads. When a tag is made of a member on an opposing team – removing one hand from a head or tail to make the tag – the person who is tagged automatically becomes a member of the team that just "caught" them.

Loyalties may swap many times in a game. It continues until everyone swears allegiance to the same team, or it seems that most people are pooped!

Variation

Toss a coin in the middle of the field, and shout the heads or tails outcome. The team which is announced chases the other team. Play several quick rounds. The game continues until everyone is caught.

JUST LIKE ME TAG

A good variation of Heads & Tails Tag that stands on its own

AT A GLANCE
Everyone places their hands on one part of their body, and attempts to tag other people for their team, obliging all tagged people to place their hands on the same part of the body as their tagger.

WHAT YOU NEED
A large, flat open space with boundaries
Minimum of 10 taggers
5 – 10 minutes

WHAT TO DO
Much like Heads & Tails Tag, instruct your group to spread out evenly throughout the playing space. Explain that on "Go," everyone is required to place their two hands onto one appropriate part of their anatomy, such as their heads, ears, shoulders, tummy, etc. This position identifies each person with his or her team. As everyone is "It" at the same time, the object is for every person to tag anyone who is not on their "team," i.e., anyone who has not placed their hands on the same part of the body. In most cases, this is pretty much the majority.

As soon as a tag is made, the tagee is obliged to transform and place their hands onto that part of the body their tagger proudly displays. So, if I am tagged by a woman who has her hands on her nose, I do the same with my hands (on my nose, not hers!). This means that the next person I tag will place their hands on their nose too. One more for my team…yay!

The action continues until everyone ends up on the same team. It will take some minutes, but if there is sufficient patience and energy, it's worth waiting for the anatomical winner! Otherwise, cut it and take a vote.

Variation

Limit the anatomical possibilities, such as "only on your head" or "above your waist."

HUG TAG

A quick warm-up that invites people to embrace one another with enthusiasm

AT A GLANCE
People avoid being tagged by engaging in a mutual hug with another person.

WHAT YOU NEED
A flat, open space with boundaries
Minimum of 10 huggers
10 – 15 minutes

WHAT TO DO
Ask your group to spread themselves across an area that has clearly marked boundaries. On this occasion, rather than looking for a volunteer to become "It," assume this role yourself and explain that you've "got no friends." This is just a little flourish I take on with the delivery of this tag, and it's not important. But as a further element of fun, I may wear a hopelessly-out-of-fashion floppy hat and suggest that my mother knitted it for me! Everyone has a real reason to run away from me now.

No prizes for guessing what's next. On "Go," everyone scatters to the wind, with several methods of escape at their disposal. They may run faster than "It," but this doesn't work for everyone. Or, preferably, they can embrace another member of the group in a mutual hug, i.e., where both people choose or at least know they are being involved in a hug. When two people are "hugging," they cannot be tagged. However, a hug is only safe for three seconds, after which, each of the hugees must detach, and rejoin the skirmish.

Note: the "It" cannot hover around people in the midst of a hug waiting to tag them as soon as they detach. That's called cheating, or "the fun is over here where we are."

Variations
- Introduce two or more "Its" to increase the energy and interaction of the game.
- If you are working with a mixed group, explain that a "safe" hug can only occur between two parties of the same or different (depending on your goals) teams, genders, nationalities, family, etc.

LEMONADE

It's Charades with a chasey twist.

AT A GLANCE
One team faces another team miming an occupation. As soon as the first team correctly guesses their trade, they will chase the second team back to their safe area.

WHAT YOU NEED
A large, flat and open space, with boundaries
Minimum of 12 trades-people
10 – 15 minutes

WHAT TO DO
Mark two "safe" areas approximately 30 metres (approximately 100 feet) apart, and a line which represents the mid-point between the two areas. Then divide your group in half.

Ask the members of each team to stand side-by-side, and face the other team about three metres (ten feet) apart. One team moves forward one step and calls out "It's as easy as Lemonade" (there's a beat to it). The other team responds by marching forward one step "Show us your trade if you're not afraid." Okay, we're now through with the preliminaries.

Upon this taunt, the "lemonade" team will immediately start to mime or "charade" a pre-determined occupation or trade. This has been agreed to earlier in the game when you asked this team to huddle and discuss which one occupation they would all like to "be" for the first round. Trades such as carpenters, hair-dressers, nurses, judges, lumberjacks, etc are all good examples.

The observing team is now charged

with a responsibility of guessing what the chosen occupation is. Anyone can guess at any time, so long as the guesses are loud and clear. As soon as the trades-people hear a correct answer, they will turn around and retreat to their safe area. Naturally, the guessers will spring into action and attempt to tag as many of the trades-people as possible. All successful tags oblige that trades-person to switch teams.

Note, lepidoptery is a fine occupation, but to be fair, no one is ever going to guess this. So in the interests of time, I suggest you coach your group to exercise a modicum of fair play. Otherwise, you'll be there forever trying to guess what the heck people who work with winged-insects are called.

Also, you may ask why "lemonade." I don't have an answer – it just is!

Variations

- Same deal, but each team charades a trade at the same time. First correct answer to identify the trade of an opposing team will spark the chase.
- Ask the teams to charade animals, sports, nationalities, etc.

GIANTS WIZARDS & ELVES

A popular tag activity that promotes a sense of community

AT A GLANCE
Two teams of people line up facing each other, and on "Go," physically demonstrate one of three prescribed characters to determine who chases the other back to their safe zone.

WHAT YOU NEED
A large, flat and open space with boundaries
Minimum of 12 people
10 – 15 minutes

WHAT TO DO
First up, identify two "safe" areas approximately 30 metres (approximately 100 feet) apart, and a line that represents the mid-point between the two areas. Then divide your group into two, roughly even teams.

With both teams gathered around you, share any story you care to spin about three shadowy figures called the giants, wizards and elves. For each character, demonstrate three distinct physical representations, such as:

Giants: Arms held high above your head, give a load scary "roaaarrr."

Wizards: One foot in front of the other and arms extended forward with fingers held in spell-like twitches, you say "Buzzzzzz" as if casting a hex.

Elves: Bend your knees slightly and hold your ears in your hands while squeaking, "Elf, elf, elf, elf."

As you perform these actions, it's a good idea to invite your group to join in - not only will it foster enthusiasm,

but you'll look pretty silly doing them on your own.

Now explain the order of things – much like "Rock, Paper Scissors" – every character is ranked higher than one but lower than another. If you describe the ranking in terms of the relative size of the characters – giants chase wizards, wizards chase elves and elves are sneaky enough to chase giants – the ol' grey matter will appreciate it.

Each group is then instructed to huddle in their respective safe areas, and agree on which one character their team would like to "be" in the first round. This will be plan A, and for the just-in-case, ask them to also agree on a Plan B, i.e., if their first chosen character is the same as the other team.

Okay, now we're getting to the exciting part. After 30 seconds of huddle-

time, each team gathers (often spread out side by side) to face the other team about half-a-metre (approximately two feet) back from the mid-point line. On the count "1, 2, 3," each team simultaneously reveals their character. Unless both teams chose the same character (in which case, you quell the anxious giggles, and call for Plan B), one team will quickly discover, to their horror, that they are about to be chased.

Each member of the chasing team attempts to tag a retreating group member before the latter crosses the line of their safe area. If a successful tag is made, the tagee is obliged to switch teams. The object is to win as many members of the other team as possible. Play continues through the cycle of huddle-reveal-chase for as many rounds as you choose, or until one team "wins."

Variation

Create three different characters representing what and whoever you like, e.g., moose, hunter and greenie!

EVERYBODY'S IT

One of the most classic tag games of all time.

AT A GLANCE
On "Go," everyone is "It."

WHAT YOU NEED
A large, flat open space with boundaries
Minimum of 10 "Its"
5 – 10 minutes

WHAT TO DO
This tag is dedicated to all those folks out there who, like me, have experienced the ignominy of being "It" for a long period of time, i.e., you never realised just how long the lunch recess was – every day! Now that I make up the rules, everyone is going to be it!

It's quite simple really. Start by having the group spread throughout the open space, and say, "Go." This will impel everyone into a frenzy of contest and self-preservation as they try to tag others whilst avoiding being tagged themselves. A compassionate contact made with one's hand on another's shoulder or back is a sufficient tag. Suggest that as soon as a tag is made, the tagee is obliged to simply crouch down in that spot to indicate to all others that he or she is "out." The action continues until the last person remains.

If they are like me, most people will be "out" within ten seconds – which doesn't necessarily make for a fun time. So, I recommend that you don't give the "winner" much time to celebrate or be lauded. Instead, surprise everyone with a sudden "Go" and it starts all over again.

Oh, here's my advice for the standard "what happens when two people tag each other at the same time?" question, which is really the same as, "I tagged him / her first, but they won't go out" complaint! The people involved have two options. One, they can both declare themselves "out" and wait for the next round, or two, they can argue for the next minute or two and miss all the fun around them.

Variations

- In the moment of contest, if a person takes a backward step, they are deemed "out." Ruthless, I know!
- While crouched down, an "out" person can tag the passing feet and legs of those folks who still survive (note, stress that only tags are permitted, no grabbing). This action will cause the tagged person to go "out" as well, and, if you want to introduce a little longevity to the game, entitle the tagger to return to the action.
- See Hospital Tag for an enduring progression of this form of tag.

HOSPITAL TAG

About as good as any tag game I know

AT A GLANCE
While attempting to tag other people, a person will place a hand on each of the first two areas of their body that have been tagged by another player, and remain in the game until they are tagged a third time.

WHAT YOU NEED
A large, flat open space with boundaries
Minimum of 10 paramedics
5 – 10 minutes

WHAT TO DO
This tag is a great extension of Everybody's It in that it gives the original a longer life time, which is awesome for people like me who hate getting out too quickly.

Do the normal "spreading" of your group. On "Go," every person is "It," that is to say, everyone is the chaser and chasee at the same time. There will be a flurry of activity as each person works frantically to tag and avoid being tagged.

Now, unlike the standard garden-variety tag, everyone in this game has three lives. When a person gets tagged for the first time, they get to live another day – but they are obliged to place one of their hands on the area of their body that got tagged, i.e., as if applying first aid to that spot. For example, if a person is tagged on their shoulder, they must place one of their hands on this shoulder, leaving only their other hand to continue the task of tagging others. Heaven help you if you get tagged on

placed on this spot, yet this person will remain in the game; but typically not for long. Without the defence offered by the hands, one is left vulnerable to all other hand-enabled taggers. However, just for the fun of it, these "dead-people walking" are still entitled to tag others, but only using their hips, i.e., siding up to another with hip extended forward to tag another before they get tagged. It's a gorgeous thing, until the fateful third tag is delivered and the hipster is "out" and obliged to crouch down.

A word of caution...I have found on occasions that when faced without the use of their hands, some folks will resort to using their feet, or put simply, kick others in an attempt at tagging. Make it quite clear, that this is not on.

the knee, or even worse, your foot!

The game continues and a second tag is applied. The other hand is then

Variations

- Entitle each person to more or less than three lives, regardless of the number of hands they possess.
- See Everybody's It for two equally applicable variations.

DEAD ANT TAG

A crazy tag that involves a little cooperation

AT A GLANCE
Upon being tagged, a person is obliged to lie on his or her back with arms and legs extended into the air, and wait to be lifted by others to a designated spot, at which point they can return to the game.

WHAT YOU NEED
A large, flat open space with boundaries

Minimum of 10 ants

5 – 10 minutes

WHAT TO DO
Make up whatever story you care to tell your group (e.g., "Someone has just kicked off the top of an ant nest and all of the ants are now frantically searching for their home.") and then spread your ants all about your space. Clearly designate one or more areas as "ant farms."

Ask for a volunteer who would like to be "It" first, and on "Go," this person will run around trying to tag everybody else. Pretty basic set up so far.

Explain that when a person is tagged, the taggee is obliged to suddenly drop to the ground and, lying on his or her back, wiggle arms and legs into the air exclaiming, "dead ant, dead ant" ad nauseam. This will act as an emergency signal to all other still-in-the-game ants to rescue one of their own. These paramedic ants (no more than four) will grab one or more limbs of the dead ant, and lift them gently to the safety of the closest "ant farm." As long as the paramedic ants remain in contact with the dead ant, they can not be tagged by "It," i.e., this is just one incentive to save souls.

Upon being gently placed (notice, I have used the word gently twice now!) onto the spot of the ant farm, the dead ant will experience a miraculous recovery and swing back into the game. And so it goes.

Variations

- For really large groups, introduce two or more ants.
- Designate an area that is somewhat peripheral to the action – representing an "abandoned picnic." Each ant is now called to visit the picnic – eating the scraps, so to speak – as many times as possible, by placing any part of its body inside the designated area. For each visit, the group gets a nominal point (or crumb), and collectively the group will work to earn as many points as possible. Of course, they must continue to save lost souls in the process.
- Just for the fun of it, call "dead ants" anywhere, anytime (i.e., long after you have played), and watch as people just drop to the floor and wiggle their way through an impulsive "dead ant, dead ant" chorus.

BASKETBALL COURT TAG

A great tag game for any area that has a basketball court

AT A GLANCE
A standard tag game, except that the movement of the chasers and chasees is restricted to the lines of a basketball court

WHAT YOU NEED
A basketball court with clearly marked lines, indoors or outdoors
Minimum of 10 people
5 – 10 minutes

WHAT TO DO
Standing on the painted lines of a basketball court, have your group spread out so that most if not all lines have at least one occupant. If you have a small group, perhaps limit the action to just the half court. Ask for a volunteer to start as the first "It," and you've got everything you need.

Each person in their attempts to tag or avoid being tagged can only travel along the lines of the court. They cannot jump from one line to another, or cut corners. It's as if they were a train, and can only steam along the designated tracks, in this case, the painted lines. As soon as a tag is accomplished, the two parties switch roles, and the action starts up again. To be fair, it is considered good manners not to re-tag the most recent tagger.

Variations
- Introduce two or more taggers, and watch the "you-can't-get-away" strategies develop.
- Consider other forms of tag games on a basketball court. Good examples include Hug Tag, Just Like Me Tag, Everybody's It and Hospital Tag.
- Same game, different court – try tennis, volleyball, netball, etc.

NAME TAG

A complex but highly-skilled name game and tag all in one

AT A GLANCE
Upon being tagged, a person must immediately call out the name of another person in the group to become the next "It" – otherwise, he or she will lose one of their three lives. The latter must tag another as quickly as possible.

WHAT YOU NEED
A flat open space with boundaries
Minimum of 10 people
10 – 20 minutes

WHAT TO DO
Clearly designate an open, yet not too expansive area. Invite everyone to start

mingling about the area, but not faster than normal walking speed. Explain that everyone will start the game with three "lives." Upon inviting one person to volunteer as the "It," the chase begins.

Upon being tagged, a tagee must quickly call out the name of another person in the group who is still "alive" and is not the person who just tagged them. There is no need to time how long a person has to call out a name – you just get a sense for when someone is stalling.

As soon as a name is called, the person whose name has been called will immediately assume the mantle of "It," and the name-caller returns to their paranoid state of tag-avoidance. All being well, the process will repeat itself over and over – a tag is made, a name is called, a tag is made, a new name is called, etc. The game continues, with people who have lost three lives removing themselves from the action, until the final three people are left circling each other.

Now, how does one lose a "life"? There are three basic outs: the just-been-tagged doesn't call out a name; the just-been-tagged calls out the name of their tagger or someone who is "out" of the game; or finally, when the tagger calls out a name and tags someone else (you'll be surprised how often this happens).

The set-up and first few minutes of play will appear confusing to some folks, but you can boil the whole game down to two rules – when tagged, call out the name of another person immediately, and when your name is called, try to tag someone as soon as possible.

....um Tom

TRUST EXERCISES

Trust is a fragile thing, and should be developed slowly and purposefully. While trust is involved in every activity of a program, a series of dedicated trust exercises can provide an opportunity for group members to rely on their physical and emotional well-being at a higher level.

Trust exercises will be safe and effective if they feature:

- A graduated series of activities that involve risk-taking at many levels
- Support and cooperation of all group members
- Fun, but some fear (of the unknown) as well

Partner Trust Exercises

Pairs Compass Walk
Come To Me
Hug A Tree
Human Camera
Spot The Difference

Group Trust Exercises

Hog Call
Look-Up Look-Down
Don't Laugh At Me
Funny Walk
The Gauntlet
I Trust You, But...
Trust Wave
Slice & Dice
Coming & Going Of The Rain

Spotting Skills Sequence

Palm Off
Trust Leans
Wind In The Willows
Levitation

A word about spotting

In this chapter, I introduce a term referred to as "spotting." Spotting is the activity of securing and protecting the physical well-being of a person engaged in an activity. In practice, it may look like breaking or catching a person's fall, but it may also be as simple as being alert for potentially harmful events or objects.

As a program develops, the momentum to assume bigger challenges – that is, greater perceived and actual risks – often increases. This may attract an individual or group to assume more physically demanding and harmful activities. Naturally, we are called to facilitate a safe outcome on these occasions, but there is enormous value in empowering our groups to partner us in this responsibility. This is where spotting skills come in.

Spotting is perhaps one of the most difficult tasks to teach because, in most cases, people do not recognise the importance of being a spotter until it's too late, i.e., someone falls or is hurt. It's a bit like shutting the gate after the horse has bolted.

Here are some key aspects to remember when teaching effective spotting skills:

- A safe spotting stance will require the spotter to be balanced with one foot in front of the other, knees flexed to absorb impact, eyes forward, arms bent at the elbow and hands up in a ready position.

- A series of common calls or commands are recommended to prepare everybody before action, such as:

  "Are you ready?"… "Yes, I am ready."

  "I'm ready to walk (run, fall, whatever)"…"Walk (run, fall, whatever) away."

- Spotters will follow and mimic the movements of the participant, and remain with them until the activity is over.

- Spotting should focus on "breaking" or supporting a fall, not catching a person.

- The head, neck and upper torso are the highest priorities for a spotter.

- Spotting is not helping or assisting the participant to complete the task.

The activities listed under the heading Spotting Skills Sequence will introduce a number of fun and fully functional activities to help you teach good spotting skills.

PAIRS COMPASS WALK

Marvel at people's amazing ability to completely lose their sense of direction.

AT A GLANCE
A blindfolded person attempts to walk in a straight line toward a target about 50 metres (approximately 160 feet) away.

WHAT YOU NEED
A wide, open but not necessarily flat space
Minimum of 2 people
10 – 20 minutes

WHAT TO DO
Ask your group to divide into pairs. To start, one person identifies a distant object from across the space – a tree, a rock, a door, etc. – and announces the object to their partner. With their eyes completely closed (no peeking), they begin to move directly toward it. Their aim is to walk "straight" to the object, in pursuit of the lofty ideals of accurate distance and direction.

To ensure a safe arrival, the sighted partner follows the blinded silently from behind. They cannot verbally or physically assist their partner, rather their role is to prevent them from encountering any "unplanned" obstacles by stopping them just short of a collision, i.e., they are a spotter. To this end, it may seem to make more sense to protect one's partner from the front or side, but in my experience, this practice tends to crookedly influence the blind person's direction and is therefore not recommended.

This activity works best if the targets are at least 50 – 100 metres (160 – 330 feet) away. Instruct the "spotters" to observe and note the tendency of their partners to veer either left or right, and to what extent. The looks on people's faces when they discover how far off they have come from their target is worth bottling. Full circles are not uncommon.

Follow up with a good-natured discussion about what helped and hindered the process of travelling to the target and the consequential development of trust. A typical result – if your compass says to go one way, and your gut feeling strongly suggests another, trust the compass!

COME TO ME

A great trust-building activity that sharpens our hearing and nerves of steel

AT A GLANCE
A sighted person attempts to approach a blindfolded person from an agreed distance and tap them on the shoulder before being detected.

WHAT YOU NEED
A wide open space, preferably outdoors
Minimum of 2 people
10 – 20 minutes

WHAT TO DO
Divide your group into pairs, perhaps using a random partner-generating category like "find someone who has the same number of letters in his or her first name that you do." Instruct everyone to scatter evenly across the area with plenty of space between partnerships, standing at least ten metres (30 feet) from one another.

In turn, one person closes his or her eyes, and calls, "Come to me" to their partner. This signal invites the sighted person to creep as quietly as they can toward their "blinded" partner. The creeper has exactly two minutes to gently tap the partner's shoulder before being detected. The jolt of shock from the blindfolded person when his or her partner makes a successful (albeit, unanticipated) tap is a real hoot.

If the "blind" person believes that he/she can hear their partner approaching, they can point in the direction (distance notwithstanding) of where they think they are. They are limited to a maximum of five attempts to reveal the whereabouts of their partners. Upon a successful detection, that round is over, and they swap roles.

Variation
Same scenario, but the creeper needs to touch the partner as quickly as possible without detection.

HUG A TREE

Excellent activity to promote an appreciation of one's environment, as well as trust

AT A GLANCE
A sighted person leads a blindfolded partner to an object, allows him or her to touch it, smell it, etc. and then after returning to the start, removes the blindfold and instructs them to locate the object.

WHAT YOU NEED
An open space, preferably outdoors
Minimum of 2 huggers
10 – 20 minutes

WHAT TO DO
In partners, one person at a time is "blind-folded," and physically guided to an object that is at least 40 – 50 metres (approximately 130 – 160 feet) away. If outdoors, trees are ideal because of their unique characteristics, but any object is fine provided it has some degree of distinctiveness about it. Once introduced, the blindfolded person may

spend up to a minute getting acquainted with the object. Encourage the use of the auditory, olfactory as well as tactile senses.

The sighted person guides the blindfolded person to the starting point, and the object for the "blind" person is to unearth and identify the object with their eyes open. Obviously, the sighted persons should not provide any clues as to the location of the secret object, but simply accompany their partners.

Ideally, the sighted person should choose a confusing route with plenty of turns, so that the "blind" person may become somewhat disoriented. The route back to the starting position should be equally confusing. Also, the experience is enriched if the object has some peculiar characteristics; for example, a tree with a hollow or a low branch, to assist the "blind" person to identify and distinguish it from other like objects.

Variation

Repeat the activity in groups of three people, in which two co-joined people are blindfolded at the same time. Tales of differing opinion often occur regarding distance, direction and the identification of the object.

HUMAN CAMERA

A wonderfully creative exercise that builds trust gently

AT A GLANCE
Sighted persons lead their blindfolded partners to three distinct objects, inviting them to open their eyes very briefly to capture a series of desired images in their mind's eye.

WHAT YOU NEED
A wide, open space
Minimum of 2 photographers
10 – 20 minutes

WHAT TO DO
Have you run out of methods to divide your group into pairs yet? Try this – ask each person in your group to find a partner who puts their shoes on in the same sequence, i.e., left on first, right on first. Or, if you want to be really fussy, divide into more distinct cate-

gories such as whether you do one sock at a time, and if so, which one first, or both socks then shoes, etc.

Now that everyone has partners, explain that one person will begin with their eyes closed, and their sighted partner will guide them physically around the designated area to focus their "camera" on three distinct objects. At each object, the sighted person will physically guide their "camera" to look in the desired direction and verbally direct all of the other settings. For example, describe the "exposure" as the desired length of time (in split seconds) you want the blinded partner to open their eyes. The "focus" will be signalling how close or far away the human lens should expect to extend their gaze as soon as their

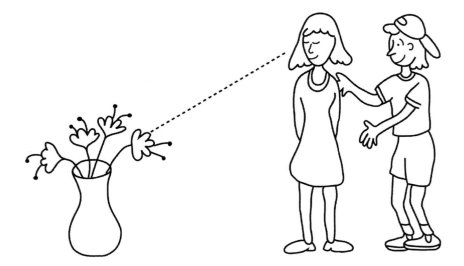

eyes open, and so on. Have some fun with it.

The blindfolded people keep their blindfolds on or their eyes closed at all times, except for when they are taking the snapshots. Their object is to retain a vivid image of each Kodak moment, to be discussed later with either their partner or as a large group. Provide an opportunity for each person to share what they saw in each "photograph," and then switch roles.

It is astonishing to see the level of detail a person can pick up in just a split second. Be prepared for some wonderful sharing, and possible links to effective communication and relationships.

Variation

Invite teams of pairs to view exactly the same objects with similar apertures, exposures and foci, and then before a switch, discuss what images each of the blindfolded people captured.

SPOT THE DIFFERENCE

An activity about noticing what's different about another

AT A GLANCE

In pairs, partners take turns altering a set number of things about their appearance, and then inviting the other to identify those changes.

WHAT YOU NEED

An open space
Minimum of 2 people
5 – 10 minutes

WHAT TO DO

Noticing the little things about people can develop trust and connection. This knowledge and a discussion of the impact the little things have on the effectiveness of a group can help to move a group forward.

Separate your group into pairs, and invite each of them to stand with their back to the other. Taking turns, one person will agree to alter three things about his or her physical appearance, e.g., roll up sleeves, swap an earring to the other ear, and untie a shoe-lace. When ready, both partners will turn to face each other and the "unaltered" person will try to identify every change in their partner's appearance. They then switch roles. At first, this is a relatively simple task.

Now, without notice, ask each partnership to repeat the exercise, but this time, altering a further three (or whatever number you desire) physical effects of their appearance. The odds are your group will groan as they cry out they can't think of anything else to change. But that's not true. They just haven't thought about it thoroughly. For example, note how many people do not think to alter their facial expression, or if they did, how many of their partners were focused on material changes and missed the bigger than usual smile or frown.

You could go even further and suggest the thoughts of a person could change too. All of these tangible and intangible effects make a big difference to a group's process.

Variation

Same deal, but join two or more pairs together, and invite half of the group to alter their appearance at a time. This time, the "unaltered" half have to agree on

HOG CALL

A grand excuse to make a lot of noise, perfect as a follow-on from a line-up

AT A GLANCE
Starting from two ends of a wide space, two lines of blindfolded people approach each other calling out an agreed word or sound in an effort to locate their partners.

WHAT YOU NEED
A large, flat and open space
Minimum of 12 people
10 minutes

WHAT TO DO
Ask your group to form a line. Alternatively, you may choose to follow on from any end-up-standing-in-a-line activity, such as Mute Line-Up. Now, fold the line in the middle so that each end faces the other. Everybody should be facing one other person, to form a pair. If you have an odd number, simply create a group of three people which should have formed at the fold of the line.

Explain that you would now like each pair to think of a matching set of words or sounds, such as peanut-butter, coca-cola, salt-pepper, etc. In addition, each person should choose one of the words or sounds as their own. After a moment, ask each pair to announce their word(s) to the group. This will allow everybody to enjoy the humour of the more inventive selections, as well as ensure that there are no duplications.

Indicate that each line represents a group that will move to opposite ends of the space. When they get there, each person will turn away from their partner and close their eyes. Have you

got the idea yet? Once all eyes are shut, ask each person to mix themselves about at their end (without turning around to locate their partner). Also, to keep people safe, ask everyone to place their hands in front of their chests with palms facing forward, elbows in, to ward off potentially harmful encounters.

Eyes closed, hands up, turn around and go! The object is to have each person find their partner by shouting their partner's "word." For example, if I am "peanut," I would yell "butter" over and over until my partner and I found each other.

When the pairs finally find one another, invite them to open their eyes and enjoy watching the melee of hog-calling around them. It is customary to applaud the final two people when they discover each other.

Variations

- Use animals. At first, the pairs do not see what's coming, but the laughs begin when they discover they have to identify themselves with a sound. The fish and the giraffes are always the last ones to find each other!
- Use words that are significant and / or relevant to your group, such as positive attributes of the organisation, or strengths of the team, etc. In this case, partners will share the same word.
- If you are in a location where shouting would be disruptive, try the whisper method. Ask participants to find each other, as above, but this time only whispering their words / sounds. It's ludicrous, functional and funny.

LOOK UP – LOOK DOWN

An awesome energiser, and a gentle introduction to trust

AT A GLANCE
People stand in a circle, looking up and down as instructed, and forming a partnership through a mutual glance.

WHAT YOU NEED
An open space for a circle
Minimum of 10 lookers
2 – 5 minutes.

WHAT TO DO
Have you ever looked blankly across a space, perhaps walking along the street, and stolen a quick glance in someone's direction? Did you glance back again only to discover that the stranger was still looking at you? These spooky encounters are what this game is all about.

Form a circle facing inwards, inviting people to place their arms on the shoulders of their neighbours, kind of like a loose huddle. Explain to your group that you are going to give a series of commands to look up and look down, one after the other. On the command "Look down," everyone is asked to cast their eyes down at the ground, some-

where in the middle of the circle. And then, on your command to "Look up," everyone is obliged to lift their gaze to the eye level of other group members.

Now, if two people happen to look at each other (i.e., by chance) at the same time, they instantaneously implode (arms fly madly into the air with exclamations of joy), break away from their neighbours, and depart the circle. This implosion will take a few seconds to settle down, at which point the circle rejoins, and the next call of "Look down" is issued.

Typically, the dearly departed members of the group just form a new circle, and continue looking up and down ad nauseam. Your group can continue to form new circles, or choose to re-join an existing one – it doesn't matter. After a minute or two, the excitement should have peaked, and you can happily move on.

Variations

- Start by looking up, then looking down directly into the eyes of another.
- Use this method to generate random partners, i.e., comprising the two people who look at each other.
- Start with two circles. As mutual looking partners implode, they simply join the other circle, back and forth, back and forth.

DON'T LAUGH AT ME

A nonsensical trust exercise that will leave you rolling on the floor with laughter

AT A GLANCE
People lie on the floor with their heads resting on the stomachs of their neighbours, attempting to pass a "laugh" down the line.

WHAT YOU NEED
A comfortable open space for people to lie down
Minimum of 8 and up to 15 people
10 – 15 minutes

WHAT TO DO
Start with one person lying on the ground, facing the ceiling or sky. If your space is limited, it is best to place this person somewhat near a corner or wall. Ask for a second person to lie down at a right angle to the first person, placing his or her head on the first person's stomach, i.e., given a bird's eye view, their bodies should form a T shape. A third person lies down, laying his or her head on the second person's stomach, and so on it goes, until you have formed one continuous line of bodies.

Already, people will be laughing, but here comes the fun bit. The first person is instructed to call out, "Ha," as in the jocular "Ha ha ha". Straight after, the second person calls out "Ha ha," and the third person issues a "Ha ha ha," and I think you get the idea. With groups of ten or more people, you can soon expect this ripple of jocularity to reverberate all over the place, and typically not in sequence.

The effort required from one's diaphragm to issue forth a "Ha," or better still, a "Ha ha ha ha ha…" will cause the head of the person lying on it to bounce about setting off this person to laugh uncontrollably because it's such a weird sensation. The more one

person laughs, the more reason the person lying on the other's stomach is compelled to laugh, and so it goes on down the line.

The "official" objective is to make it all the way down the line calling out the "Ha's" in sequence without stopping or interrupting. But, of course, this is rarely possible, and should never really be your goal.

Variations

- You can place two people's heads at right angles off one person's stomach, forming a cross of sorts.
- Invite people to recite some nonsensical tongue twister such as "unique New York" to produce even more side-splitting jollity. Hehehe, I just laughed typing it!!

FUNNY WALK

A gradual building up of trust to look silly in front of others

AT A GLANCE
People are invited to walk in the most ridiculous manner they know back and forth from one side of a space to the other several times in different configurations.

WHAT YOU NEED
A flat, open space to accommodate a line of people
Minimum of 10 people
5 – 10 minutes

WHAT TO DO
Designate one area from which your group will start, and another to which your group will move. Starting from behind the first line, gather your group and explain that you would like each person to walk independently from here to the other side. It's a good idea for you to cross the area first playing absolutely full-out, to spark your group's imaginations.

Then, upon arriving at your destination (having soaked up all the titters along the way), invite everyone else to follow you. Explain that each person must attempt to walk in a way that no one else has ever performed before. Also, to quell any "people-will-look-at-me" concerns, encourage your group to walk across the area at the same time, or whenever they are ready to go.

Once everyone has crossed, step up the challenge and ask them to find a partner, and cross back to the other side, but this time joined physically with the other. Upon this second crossing, two pairs join forces to form a group of four, and repeat the process, each time inventing an all-together-never-been-seen-before funny walk. As you can guess, the expanding walks culminate in the entire group crossing jointly in one final celebratory walk to the finish line.

THE GAUNTLET

A terrific tactile activity you can use to reinforce critical spotting skills

AT A GLANCE
A person walks between two lines of people acting as "spotters," falling in any direction and at any time to test the reaction and catching skills of their group.

WHAT YOU NEED
A flat, open space
Minimum of 10 people
10 – 15 minutes

WHAT TO DO
It's always a good idea to reinforce the learning of your group. This activity is designed specifically to reinforce effective "spotting" skills, but is also a wonderful tactile exercise to sharpen your group's focus and have a little fun in the process.

Split your assembly into two smaller groups, and ask each group to stand in a straight line facing the other about one to one and a half metres (three and a half to five feet) apart. There should be a lovely straight corridor between the two lines of spotters.

This is one of those activities which I believe is useful for you, as the facilitator, to demonstrate first. Standing at

Spotters ready

appear as if everything is "cool," and then, without warning, suddenly lean or fall to any one of the 360 degrees around you. The group's object is to catch your fall, and then prop you upright to resume your journey. Explain to the group that it is not their job as spotters to keep the walker upright at all times, rather it is to simply to be there when they fall (in any direction), and return them to equilibrium.

The reason you should go first is to "test" your group if and when you choose to fall backwards or forwards – the two most likely directions your group may not be prepared for. One of two results will occur. One, you will be effectively spotted, which is good news for everyone. Or two, you fall flat on your butt, which is not so good, but you are prepared for this possibility and manage to break your fall. This second consequence will rapidly focus your group, and is why I recommend you do not invite a participant to go first, for the just-in-case they are not caught.

one end of the corridor, issue a series of agreed commands (e.g., "Spotters Ready / *Ready* / Ready to Walk / *Walk Away*") back and forth to prepare and focus your group, and then walk slowly through the middle of the spotters.

Your object, as the walker, is to

As soon as a person exits, the exercise is over, i.e., no smartie pants should attempt to feign a fall beyond this point. Do this exercise as often as you feel necessary.

Variations

- With young people, suggest that they are very tired and wonky on their feet, and for adults, they are walking home from the pub. Observe the fun index sky-rocket.
- Do it blind-folded.

I TRUST YOU, BUT...

A classic trust exercise which is as much fun to watch as it is to play.

AT A GLANCE
Starting from a distance of about 50 metres (165 feet), a blind-folded person runs at three-quarter pace toward a long line of spotters.

WHAT YOU NEED
A large, flat and open space
Minimum of 10 spotters
15 – 20 minutes

WHAT TO DO
Ask for a volunteer to be the first "runner," and while they tramp up to one end of your space about 50 metres (165 feet) away, align the rest of your group into one long line of "spotters" about arms-length apart from one another at the opposite end.

Once your spotters are in place and the "runner" is blindfolded, ask for the runner to initiate a series of agreed-upon calls to prepare everyone for their assault. On "Ready!", the runner will raise their hands out in front of them (about chest height) and run directly for the line of spotters. Given that they are blindfolded, it is recommended that you instruct your runners to travel at three-quarter pace only. A walk would be pointless, but a full-out sprint could prove dangerous.

This is what's supposed to happen. The spotters will keep a vigilant eye on the runner, with their hands up in front of them ready to meet the hands (not the body) of the runner as soon as he / she arrives. Using their hands and arms as a "spring" will soften the halting process which is preferable to stopping the runner by colliding with their torso. Also, the spotters should keep as silent

as possible, even when they have to adjust their position left or right, so the runner is not given any clues as to where the end of the space is.

Ideally, the runners will keep moving at an even pace at all times, even when they think they have come to the end of the space. Typically, and in the interests of self-preservation, most runners will slow down a little, if not stop completely when they think they have approached or passed the end. In a perfect world, they will not slow down or open their eyes until they have been stopped by their spotters.

There are always a ton of things to share at the end of this exercise, so allow ample time for a discussion of what it means to trust, how it felt to be the runner, why people slowed down, etc.

If you have a small group of say ten people, spread the group out but clearly instruct them to move left or right so that the runner will always come into contact with at least two spotters, i.e., and not run through a gap in the line.

Variations

- Same arrangement, with the added objective of stopping when the walker / runner thinks they are just short of the end. This is bound to spark a lot of amusement as many people discover just how poor their sense of direction and distance is.
- Walk the distance.

TRUST WAVE

A dynamic run-through exercise that tests the mettle of your group

AT A GLANCE
A person runs at three quarter pace down the middle of two lines of people who hold their arms out-stretched in front of them until the very last moment before the runner passes in front of them.

WHAT YOU NEED
A wide, flat and open space
Minimum of 12 people
10 – 20 minutes

WHAT TO DO
Ask one lucky person to be the first runner and invite him or her to move about 15 to 20 metres (50 to 65 feet) away from the group. Organize the rest of your group into two straight lines, each line facing and standing about one to one and a half metres (three and a half to five feet) apart from the other. Ideally, each member of a line will stand shoulder to shoulder with their neighbours, but if you have a small group, it will work to space them about arms-length apart.

Now, instruct each person in the two lines to extend their arms out in front of them, and position their arms alternately between the people directly opposite, i.e., one person should not

have their own two arms placed next to each other. With their eyes now turned toward the runner, the runner will issue forth the agreed-upon commands, and on "Ready!" begin their run at three-quarter pace towards the entrance of the corridor between the two lines.

The object for the people in the lines is to keep their arms laid out in front of them for as long as possible. That is, they should only flick their arms up and out of the way of the runner at the very last moment before a collision with a juxtaposed nose occurs. I suggest flicking up and not down because up is way more scary as arms flash by the runner's eyes. From the side of the lines, the arms should flail up as if gripped in a wave as the runner scoots through.

Ideally, the runner is expected to maintain an even pace through the two lines and out the end, and keep his or her eyes open at all times. That's all very well in theory of course, but it's very much a different story when you actually have to be the runner.

Again, like most trust exercises, take some time with your group to reflect back on what it was like to be the "wavers" and the runner, why people slowed down, how it felt to trust the group with a physical responsibility, etc.

A safety note: it's a good idea to remove all watches and bulky jewellery from the "wavers'" arms before the runner passes through.

Variations

- Alter the height at which people lay and extend their arms, i.e., from chest height to eye-level.
- See Slice and Dice for an excellent progression.

SLICE & DICE

An exhilarating variation of the Trust Wave

AT A GLANCE
A person walks down the middle of two lines of people of who are continually swinging their arms up and down in a chopping motion, narrowly missing the walker as he or she passes by.

WHAT YOU NEED
A wide, flat and open space
Minimum of 12 people
10 – 20 minutes

WHAT TO DO
A similar set-up as the Trust Wave. First up, ask one brave person to be the initial walker. Position them at the entrance of two straight lines of people, each line facing and standing about one to one and a half metres (three and a half to five feet) away from the other.

Upon issuing the agreed safety and ready commands, the "choppers" start to swing their arms full stretch in front of them up and down in a chopping motion. For good effect, invite the choppers to make appropriate "shh-httt" and "phhhtttt" sounds as they slice and dice their way through the air. Where possible, each chopper should swing his or her arms either side of another person's arm, so that no two adjacent arms belong to one person.

Now, imagine the view held by the walker as he or she stands anxiously at the top of the lines – just awesome. The walker is then invited to walk calmly yet steadily through this veritable human "slice and dice" machine. Walkers should attempt to maintain an even pace and keep their eyes open at

all times. The choppers aim to create as much slicing action as possible within the immediate vicinity of the walker. Indeed, they are encouraged to slice right in front of the nose and eyes of the walker as they mosey through, but of course, never actually make contact. Like all good adventures, it's the perceived risk (and not the actual risk) that counts.

The pace of the walker is critical to the safety of this activity, so it's a good idea to start the walker a few metres (ten feet) back from the entrance so the choppers can gauge their initial speed.

Variations

- Uping the challenge, invite walkers to become "runners" at the recommended three-quarter pace.
- Adjust the velocity of the choppers, particularly for those faint of heart. Indeed, try a slow motion version with accentuated facial expressions just for the fun of it.

COMING & GOING OF THE RAIN

A calming way to bring closure to an activity or a group

AT A GLANCE

Standing in a circle facing one another's backs, people use their hands to replicate a series of beats and strokes that they receive on their backs to the back of the person in front of them.

WHAT YOU NEED

An open space for a tight circle
Minimum of 10 people
2 – 5 minutes

WHAT TO DO

This is a special activity so be sure to introduce your group into the 'space' of this exercise in a relaxed manner, i.e., not directly after an all-or-nothing tag game. Mimicking the sounds and the feel of a rain storm, this is a particularly rewarding activity that I save for deserving groups.

Ask your group to form a tight circle in which everyone, including yourself, is facing the back of the person in front of them. Oh, okay, while you're there, why not introduce a quick neck rub. For most groups, this activity alone will be a soothing experience, but wait – there's more.

Moving on from the neck rub, invite your group to place their hands onto the back of the person in front of them and then close their eyes. Explain that in a few moments, they will feel a series of beats and strokes on their own back, and they are then obliged to use their hands to replicate these very moves onto the back of the person in front of them. As you can guess, these moves are passed all the way around the circle, having originated from one person – in most cases, you.

Encourage your group to mirror all of the moves exactly just as soon as they are received. The tactile senses will be heading into over-drive, but so too will the auditory senses. To this end, even if a person can hear the beats changing behind them, they should still wait until they actually receive change before passing it on.

There's no right or wrong to the passing of the rain, but imagine the moves mimicking the beats and strokes of the rain falling onto the ground. It starts with a soft stroking sensation, and then little drops, building to bigger and heavier drops, until finally the full fury of the shower (not storm) is felt. And then, slowly, the showers break up a little, and turn into lighter drops again, before finally disappearing altogether. Ahhhhh....

Variations

- Invite each person in turn to create a unique "sensation" to be passed around the circle.
- Break into groups of four or five people, and invite one person to lie down while their partners create a collective and simultaneous coming and going of the rain.

PALM OFF

A terrific energiser as well as a great introduction to spotting skills

AT A GLANCE
Two people with their feet together and palms up in front of their chests, face each other at about 30cm (one foot) apart, and on "Go," try to bring one another off balance.

WHAT YOU NEED
A flat, open space for pairs to form

Minimum of 2 people
5 – 10 minutes

WHAT TO DO
Separate your group into pairs. Ask each person to stand with their own feet together, facing their partner with a gap of approximately 30cm (one foot) between the front of each other's toes.

Each person then raises their hands to chest height and turns their palms forward to face their partner.

The partners are ready to start. You could go straight into what happens next, or do as I do, and introduce a little school time fun to commence proceedings. Invite your partnerships to initiate a series of calls and claps before they engage in mortal combat – such as "and one and two and three and go," where each "and" is timed with a clap of your own hands, and each "number" is timed with a clap with your partner's hands.

On "Go," the game starts, and each person will attempt to make contact (or not) with their partner to cause them to come off balance. Stress that contact can only be made with a person's hands – no other part of the body may be touched. In many cases, a clever person will baulk a move (thereby not making contact at all) and cause the momentum of their partner to institute a fall. The thrill of avoiding a fall is infectious, so you should allow plenty of time to play several rounds.

At this point, you can simply move onto the next activity, or, if you are planning to introduce spotting skills,

initiate a short discussion. For example, I have found this activity to be a wonderful precursor for teaching spotting skills, because it demonstrates an effective (balanced) stance with two feet apart, i.e., this is what people do to recover their balance. The hands up position also indicates that a person is ready and alert, which is an essential attribute of a good spotter.

Variations

- Invite each partner to squat down on their toes to play. Each person attempts to cause the other to fall forward onto their hands or backwards onto their heels.
- Reduce the distance between the toes of the two partners, so that they are almost touching.

TRUST LEANS

The quintessential exercise to develop spotting skills and group trust

AT A GLANCE
One person leans back into the arms of a second person, and upon returning to their original standing position, may choose to repeat this process leaning further back with each attempt.

WHAT YOU NEED
A flat, open space with non-slip surface
Minimum of 2 people
10 – 20 minutes

WHAT TO DO
This is one of those activities that will focus your group on one set of skills (spotting), whilst secretly developing another (trust and empathy). The beauty is that most people don't see it coming, until they reflect on what they have just done. This step is totally recommended here.

Start by giving a demonstration of the correct procedures, before separating your group into pairs to try it out for themselves. As you are dealing with many fragile issues here, be very particular and intentional, but not overly serious. This is meant to be fun, but it is possible for people to get hurt – both physically and emotionally.

Ask for a volunteer – the faller – to stand with their back toward you, the designated spotter. Explain that they are about to lean backwards into your arms, so they should keep their body firm, and try to pivot from their ankles as they lean. Also, advise them to cross their arms in front of their chest to keep their arms and elbows out of harm's way.

Assume the correct spotter's position, call out the agreed safety commands, and then upon hearing the final call of "Fall away," the faller will lean slowly back into the arms of the spotter. Ideally, the spotter should start with their hands on the back of the faller to build confidence and to gauge for the first time the momentum and weight of the person they are supporting. Return the faller to their original standing position, repeat the calls, and this time allow the faller to lean back a little further, perhaps this time allowing for a little space between the faller's back and the spotter's ready hands.

It is possible for the faller to lean a long way back, but the fall should only go as far as the faller and / or spotter feel comfortable. Indeed, the process will continue until either the spotter or the faller chooses to stop. However, encourage people where possible to take a step beyond their comfort zone, because this is where the learning really occurs. When ready, switch roles and repeat.

Variation

Start with three people, two spotters each facing a third person – the faller – in between them. This time, the faller may lean backwards or forwards, and at any time. Generally, as the spotters support each lean, they return the faller to the centre and this momentum causes them to develop a rocking back-and-forth motion. Be sure to describe this as a gentle rocking motion, and not a tennis match! The skills required to spot the front of a person are similar to the back, but the forward spotter is advised to use the faller's crossed arms to catch their lean, i.e., to avoid embarrassing hands-on-chest issues.

WIND IN THE WILLOWS

Perfect for developing a terrific sense of care and connection with a group

AT A GLANCE
Standing in the middle of a circle of "spotters," a person will close his or her eyes and lean in all directions to be passed gently back and forth among the group.

WHAT YOU NEED
A flat, open space with non-slip surface
Minimum of 10 people
15 – 25 minutes

WHAT TO DO
Form a circle of approximately 10 to 15 spotters; any more and the circle may start to get a little too wide to be safe or effective. Invite one person to stand directly in the centre of the circle, with their feet together and arms crossed on their chest. Upon calling the agreed safety commands, the faller will close his or her eyes, and then lean slowly to one direction – it doesn't matter which way. Pivoting from the ankles, the faller should try to keep feet stationary at all times.

It's a good idea to initially pass the faller fully around the circle so that every person has an opportunity to support their wooden colleague, as well as gauge their weight and momentum. For purposes of sharing the load (read safety) it is necessary for at least two spotters to be in contact with the faller at all times.

Upon completing the initial circle and prescribed ready commands, the group may pass the faller randomly back and forth across the circle. Note, I said the word "pass," and not "fling" – this is critical. Even if the person being flung doesn't mind this behaviour, it is possible that others in the group who have not yet had a go will reconsider their decision if they do not think the group is being safe.

As the group gains confidence and competence, allow for the circle to widen slightly to afford bigger leans and falls. Let the rocking motion continue until either the faller has had enough, or about 30 to 60 seconds has elapsed. Be sure to check in with the faller at the end to hear what the experience was like. Also, what did they observe, how easy was it to fully submit to the group, etc.

Variations

- Ramping up the challenge and velocity at which a faller may travel, invite the circle of spotters to sit down using their feet and legs to form a tight circle around the feet of the faller. This position effectively locks the faller's feet into position. On "Go," the faller assumes their typical unbending stance, and the spotters raise their arms above their heads to support the falls. This option is much more dynamic, and should only be presented to highly competent spotters.
- Upon completing the typical back and forth motions, move the faller onto the Levitation.

LEVITATION

A stand-alone activity, or a wonderful add-on to Wind In The Willows

AT A GLANCE
A person with his or her eyes closed is lifted off the ground and laid horizontally by a group of spotters to shoulder height, and gently rocked back and forth before being placed back on the ground.

WHAT YOU NEED
A flat, open space with non-slip surface
Minimum of 10 people
15 – 25 minutes

WHAT TO DO
Before launching yourself into this exercise, take a look at Wind In The Willows. It's a perfect lead-up activity, but certainly not necessary, just nice.

Ask for one person to stand in the middle of a circle of people. With their feet together, arms crossed on their chest, and keeping a stiff posture, this person will join in the agreed safety commands (e.g., "Are my spotters

ready?" / "*Ready!*" / "I'm ready to fall."
/ "*Fall away!*") and then close their
eyes. On the final command, the rest
of the group will work together to lift
this person off the ground. The group
should lean the middle person backwards at first, holding their feet in
place. Then, bending their knees and
not their backs, the spotters will slip in
under the faller's legs and
upper torso and lift together to
haul their trusting colleague off the
ground.

For most occasions, lifting to shoulder
height is more than enough. It will be
accessible to all members of your
group, thereby permitting the most
number of hands to be in contact. It's
good practice to assign a dedicated person to look after the head and neck of
the "elevated" – not only are they critical anatomical bits, but are likely to
flop around uncomfortably during the
exercise if care is not taken.

At this point, silently and gently start
to initiate a rocking movement of the
body that travels in the direction of the
head, and then to the toes and back to
the head. Back and forth, back and
forth, maintain a soothing swaying sensation. After about 15 to 20 seconds,
instruct your group to sustain the rocking as long as possible, while bending
their knees and bringing their now
almost comatose colleague to lie flat on
the ground.

This is purely a style preference, but I
also like to ask my group to remain
crouched on the ground, until the person has regained their composure and
is ready to be assisted back onto their
feet. It's my belief that looking up at a
large number of people staring down
at oneself can be unsettling for some
folks.

Be prepared for all sorts of sharing
here, from the chilled-out-I-don't-know-
what-to-say to the totally ecstatic. Also
observe how many people felt that they
were being carried out of the area,
rather than rocked in place. These
folks I have dubbed "the travellers" –
as distinct from the "floaters" – and my
extensive clinical research indicates
that they make up 40 percent of the
population.

Variation

Extend the gentle "standing-upright-rocking" of Wind In The Willows with a
Levitation. Use a silent gesture to halt the group's passing, lean the faller backwards so that their head and neck can be supported, and then prepare for a lift.

GROUP PROBLEM-SOLVING EXERCISES

Group problem-solving activities, or initiatives, provide an opportunity for group members to effectively communicate, cooperate and interact with each other to solve a problem that often has more than one "answer."

These activities often stimulate significant growth for a group, especially if their experience is processed upon completion.

Initiatives typically feature the following characteristics:

- Physical and verbal interaction among group members
- High levels of arousal and excitement
- Opportunities for trust, leadership, communication and group cooperation to evolve
- Focus on the process, not just the task

Low-impact / Cognitive Group Exercises

Mute Line Up
Quick Shuffle
About Now
Group Compass Walk
Negotiation
Body English
Izzat You
Sherpa Walk
Circle Clap

High-impact Group Exercises

Magic Shoes
Everybody Up
Popsicle Push-Up
The Clock
Span The Room
Four Pointer
Don't Touch Me
Human Knot
Lap Circle

MUTE LINE-UP

One of the simplest and best methods to form a random line-up

AT A GLANCE
People communicate non-verbally to locate their spot in a straight line, formed in accordance wih a set criteria.

WHAT YOU NEED
A large, open space to accommodate a line of people
Minimum of 10 mutes
10 – 20 minutes

WHAT TO DO
Instruct your group that from this moment on they are all mute, i.e., no verbal communication whatsoever. Then explain that you would like them all to form into one straight line according to some criteria, for example, their height or date of birth. For

more ideas, check out the popular alternatives below.

There is often confusion or a series of halting questions at first because some folks simply can't stop themselves from talking, or they can't see how they can communicate without opening their mouth. Be firm, restate the problem, and continue to remind the group not to talk. A further hint: beware in your briefing of the problem not to inadvertently indicate where the start and finish of the line is, i.e., by pointing as you describe the problem. This should remain part of the problem the group needs to solve.

After some stumbling, ideas will begin to emerge and progress will slowly be made. Clapping, stomping,

drawing pictures (not words or letters) in the air all have their place as legitimate forms of primitive communication. Offer encouragement at times when it seems people are getting frustrated.

When the whole group is looking at you, the task is probably complete. Ask the group to whip down the line to evaluate the sequence, then allow a couple of minutes for the explosion of conversation that predictably occurs as a result of pent-up who-did-this and you-did-thats. Be prepared to discuss issues of effective communication, leadership and problem-solving.

Variations

- Upping the ante, ask your group to wear blindfolds to limit another useful faculty.
- Some popular line-up criterion includes shoe size, date of birth (not including the year), date of a particular event or memory, street address number, last two digits of home telephone number, distance from here, favourite animal, etc.

QUICK SHUFFLE

A good introductory, success-oriented exercise

AT A GLANCE
A group works together to re-shuffle seven people who have their eyes closed back to their original positions in a line.

WHAT YOU NEED
An open space
Minimum of 10 people
10 – 15 minutes

WHAT TO DO
Be careful not to reveal too much in this briefing, lest you give your group a clue as to what's about to happen. It's not critical, because you can always up the challenge, but it's good to preserve the adventure for as long as possible.

Ask seven people from your group to stand in one line, side-by-side, in front of the rest of your group, and then ask the latter to simply look at the former for about ten or so seconds. Now, instruct those who are doing the looking, to close their eyes for 15 to 20 seconds, during which time the chosen seven will totally shuffle their positions. No one leaves the line, each person simply moves to a new spot within it.

As you will have guessed, the group now opens their eyes and is charged with the responsibility of re-shuffling the group back to their original configuration. It is quite likely that not even the seven people will recall their original positions correctly – because they didn't see what was coming either, and that's okay.

The importance of this activity is that the looking group work together cooperatively to solve the problem. Like most initiatives, it's not always about getting the right answer. To this end, and to prevent a "hero" from doing all of the shuffling, be sure to frame this simple exercise as a "group" problem, and suggest that every "looking" person take a turn in making a shuffle, one at a time. The chosen seven should remain silent at all times during the shuffling process.

Of course, after the first round, everyone is attuned to memorising the formation of the line when the activity is repeated, but there's still plenty of room for disagreement. Naturally, applaud the idea of using pen and paper, but disallow it!

Variations

- If you have a large group, create several sets of seven, with matching groups of three to five people to do the looking and re-shuffling.
- Experiment with larger look-at-me lines, of say ten or more people.
- Moving only one person at a time, record how many moves it takes for a line to be correctly reshuffled.

ABOUT NOW

A simple guessing game

AT A GLANCE
Individuals standing as a part of their group will sit down when they estimate sixty seconds have elapsed since the starting command.

WHAT YOU NEED
A comfortable, open space for people to sit on the ground
Minimum of 10 people
A time piece with a second hand
5 – 10 minutes

WHAT TO DO
Gather your group in front of you with sufficient room for each person to sit on the ground, but don't have them sit down yet! With a time piece at the ready, instruct your group to sit down when they believe exactly 60 seconds has elapsed. Note: there is no talking permitted during the exercise, and individuals assume full responsibility for when they believe the sixty seconds have expired.

Obviously, it will be necessary for people not to look at their watches as they perform this task, i.e., if the temptation is too great, ask that all watches be removed. Also, you are well advised to check that the area you are playing in does not have a clock on the wall (but that's another story).

The time starts ticking when you call out, "Now," and off they go. It's extraordinary how quickly some people believe one minute will pass, or how long. Purely out of interest, note the person(s) who sits at or closest to the 60-second mark.

Observe how group pressure plays a part in people's decision-making

processes. It will look like corn popping in reverse – a few early sits, then a few more, then a flurry of them for an extended period, and then some late ones. And then of course, there's always a few tough, residual corns that just refuse to pop!

Variations

- Same deal, but this time the group can communicate with each other all they like, before and during the exercise, with the objective of having everyone sit at the same time. Emphasis is on seeking consensus, as well as achieving a group-sit as close to one minute as possible.
- Stand your group in a line at the edge of a wide space, and ask them to walk to the other side at a pace that will have them cross a designated line at exactly sixty-seconds.

GROUP COMPASS WALK

A whole group "blind-leading-the-blind" experience

AT A GLANCE
A blindfolded group of people attempt to walk directly in a straight line towards a target about 50 to 100 metres (165 to 330 feet) away.

WHAT YOU NEED
A wide, open but not necessarily flat space
Minimum of 10 people
15 – 30 minutes

WHAT TO DO
Take a look at Pairs Compass Walk to give you some ideas for how you may sequence your program to lead up to this group exercise.

Standing at one edge of your wide, open space, identify an object about 50 to 100 metres (165 to 330 feet) away, e.g., a tree, a door, a pole, etc that you would like your group to walk toward. Their object is simple – with their eyes closed (or blindfolds on), the group is to walk directly to the nominated target and stop just short of touching it.

The group gets just one attempt, and must remain in total physical contact with one another at all times. They will have whatever planning time you choose to give them to prepare for the task, e.g., ten minutes is cool. The group may also stop and start as often as they like once they have begun their journey, communicating all the way, but without opening their eyes.

As facilitator, stroll quietly alongside the group as they walk doggedly toward their target. Alert them to any harmful hazards along the way, stopping them just short of any danger, but requesting that they continue to keep their eyes closed to manage the situation.

When the group decides that they have arrived just short of their target, or they are about to hit it, ask everyone to release the contact they have with their group, and point in the direction they personally believe the target is situated, i.e., suggesting not everyone will concur with the group's sense of direction. Then, open your eyes. Voila!

This pointing of fingers is a moment of truth for the group. Invite everyone to look around, not only for the target, but at the directions that people are pointing toward. Questions like "Why did so many people think the target was somewhere else? Did the original plan work? and Was there a contingency?" should all spring to mind.

Variation

Although it involves props, become "Hansel & Gretel" and silently drop an easy-to-see-at-a-distance item directly behind the group as they tramp along to mark their path. This will invariably spark many "oohs" and "ahhhs," not to mention a real sense of what was happening when.

NEGOTIATION

A dynamic initiative that will spark many valuable discussion points

AT A GLANCE
Over several rounds with a view to reaching consensus, a number of small groups will meet – without ever speaking – to physically demonstrate their preferred gesture, to create one common gesture for all groups.

WHAT YOU NEED
A wide, open space with break-out areas if possible
Minimum of 12 negotiators
15 – 30 minutes

WHAT TO DO
Separate your group into three or four roughly even-numbered smaller groups. To set the scene, explain that each group will meet in a discrete corner (or break-out room), to secretly discuss and create a physical gesture that they will soon reveal to the other groups. For

example, a group may choose to stick out their tongue while waving their hands up high as their gesture du jour.

After a few minutes, invite each group to return to the centre and stand in a position where every other group can see them. On "Go," every member of every group simultaneously demonstrates their gesture for everyone to see, at the same time observing all the other gestures.

Once the giggles die down, explain that the goal of this activity is to now achieve consensus among all of the groups, by way of having every group demonstrate an identical gesture within the fewest possible rounds, i.e., shortest time frame. This common gesture may be a choice to adopt one of the initial designs, a derivative of them all, or something completely new. Who knows? When clear, the groups return

to their homes to discuss their gesture of choice for the next round.

Most importantly, the groups are not permitted to communicate with the other groups at any time throughout the "silent negotiation" process, or whilst in conversation with their own kind. Limit the rounds to eight at the most, by which time, you will have managed to stimulate lots of discussion about decision making, loyalty, letting go, communication and goal setting.

Variations

- It may meet your program goals to suggest that the gestures reflect something relatable to your group, such as "teamwork," "the meaning of life" or other themes.
- At the end of round three, permit one representative from each small group to meet in a neutral spot for two minutes to discuss anything they choose. Typically, the discussion will fall somewhere between the "do-it-this-way-or-else" and "let's-work-together" categories. Observe that agreement among these folks does not necessarily beat a path to consensus for everyone else.

BODY ENGLISH

Using a human form of written language to solve problems

AT A GLANCE
Groups of people configure their bodies specifically to physically shape the letters of a word to communicate a message to a distant group.

WHAT YOU NEED
A wide, open space

Minimum of 10 bodies
20 – 30 minutes

WHAT TO DO
Divide your gathering into smaller groups of say five to ten people. The number in each group doesn't really matter, but if you have a very large

group, ensure that you end up with an even number of groups so that you can pair them off.

Set up an area where two groups can stand at least 50 metres (165 feet) apart from each other with a clear view to the other. With a "message" in mind, each group will attempt to communicate with the opposite group in the quickest and most effective manner possible using their bodies to form the letters of the alphabet. I shouldn't have to say it, but I will – no verbal communication is permitted between the groups at any time, of course!

The message to be transmitted can be created in several ways. You may choose to make it in advance and deliver it in written or verbal form, or give your groups the freedom to develop their own. In each case, the message should provide an instruction for the other group to do something, such as "Stand on one foot singing 'Jingle Bells'" or "Build a tall tower made of shoes."

On "Go," one group will start by relaying their message one letter or word at a time, depending on their technique and the size of their number. The groups should be encouraged to be as quick as possible, but the most important factor is that the message is effective and successfully sparks the other group into action.

This exercise clearly focuses on effective communication, but issues of teamwork and perspective will also give rise to a valuable discussion.

Variation

Each group is challenged to "relay" as many four or five letter words as they can create in four minutes. In this case, the groups can be situated closer to each other so that they may shout the "word" (to check its accuracy) as they see it develop before them.

IZZAT YOU

A problematic get-to-know-you game

AT A GLANCE
People milling about in a group repeat a series of greetings to each other in an effort to return to their original positions in a circle.

WHAT YOU NEED
A flat, open space
Minimum of 10 people
10 – 15 minutes

WHAT TO DO
There are many ways you can lead up to this activity, but the bottom line is that you start with your group standing in a circle. Ask each person to greet the neighbour on their left with a laid-back "How ya goin?", and to answer the neighbour on their right with an agreeable, "Just fine thanks." Repeat these greetings several times with the requisite turning of heads.

Next, explain the 'bumper's up' position (eyes closed, hands up in front of chest with palms facing forward and elbows in), and invite everyone to mingle into the centre of the circle for a short while. With their eyes closed at all times, each person should move silently in and out of the melee using their bumpers to fend off people where necessary.

At a point when you believe the group is sufficiently mixed-up, call "Stop" and remind people to keep their eyes closed. Now, instruct everyone to find their way back into the circle exactly as they were standing a minute ago, but only using the phrases "How ya goin?" and "Just fine thanks" to guide them. Nothing else can be said or communicated.

A person will have to rely heavily on their listening senses to get them home and in the correct sequence. The object for the group is to do this as quickly, yet safely as possible. Perform the task two or three times, inviting the group to develop strategies for reducing their time between rounds.

Variation

Play King Frog at some point prior to this activity. So, when the group is appropriately mixed-up with their eyes closed, ask them to find their way back home by recalling and making whatever noise the very first animal they created made.

SHERPA WALK

A classic blindfolded activity that is steeped in tradition.

AT A GLANCE
A sighted person leads a group of people – connected to one another and blind-folded – on a journey through a series of obstacles and challenges.

WHAT YOU NEED
A wide, open, not necessarily flat space, preferably outdoors
Minimum of 8 walkers
10 – 20 minutes

WHAT TO DO
Imagine oxygen masks, walking sticks, snowshoes and heavy woollen jackets – prepare your group for a stroll through the Himalayas, or any other open terrain you care to conquer!

Before setting off, you need a sherpa, the person who will guide your group on this epic trek. Often, as facilitator, you will be the best judge of an appropriate route, but it is possible to select a member from the group. Also, it's best not to tell your group what's about to happen. Let it just occur as a progression, perhaps as a unique method to move your group from the previous activity.

Ask everyone to form a line, and grab the hand of the person in front of them, or place a hand on their shoulder, whatever is more comfortable. Everyone closes their eyes (or pulls down their blindfolds) and at your lead, prepares to follow the person in front of them.

People are permitted, indeed, encouraged to talk. Yet, I have discovered that when you remove sight, most people also lose their ability to speak! As the lead, talk frequently to the blindfolded person at the front of the line and inform them of dips in the path, overhanging shrubs, chairs to step over, etc. Most folks will realize that they should pass this information "down the line," but that doesn't always happen.

The route you choose can be short or long, arduous or gentle, it's up to you and your judgement of what would be a good fit for your group. It's useful to provide moments along the journey in which some people's comfort zones will be stretched – physically and / or emotionally. As you can imagine, many connections can be drawn from the walk to "real-life" experiences, and may form the foundation of some interesting discussion points. Some of these points may be: How did you cope when faced with an obstacle? What supports were necessary to help you succeed? and When did your communication work best?

As in life, the value of an experience is found in the journey and not necessarily the destination.

Variations
- Lead your blindfolded group members verbally, and offer no physical assistance at all.
- Separate into pairs, and invite one person to be blindfolded at a time. The sighted person leads their partner verbally (not physically) on a journey from A to B through a series of obstacles and challenges.

CIRCLE CLAP

Exploring the ability for a group to create the sound of two hands clapping

AT A GLANCE
Standing in a circle, people ready their hands in concert with their neighbours to clap simultaneously and yet create the sound of one clap.

WHAT YOU NEED
An open space
Minimum of 8 clappers
10 – 15 minutes

WHAT TO DO
Let's warm up first, to create a little excitement for the main event. Starting in a circle, ask someone to clap their hands once to set off a chain reaction of single claps which pass from person to person all the way around the group. Each clap should follow immediately after the clap before it at time-warp speed. Do it several times, time each attempt, and see if the group can break a nominal world record.

Next, suggest to your group the impulse is now going to zip around the group so fast, it will seem as if only one clap was accomplished by the whole group at the same time. Indeed, that is exactly what the group will be aiming to achieve – one solitary clapping sensation. However – and here's the catch – no one is permitted to clap their own hands together, i.e., they must fashion a clap with another person's hand. As you can imagine, this will take a little imagination, but the problem-solving normally occurs quickly.

If you feel particularly helpful, you could suggest a starting point. For example, standing in a circle, everyone places their left palm facing up towards their left neighbour, and places their right palm facing down directly above the left palm of their right neighbour.

It's all just a matter of timing then. However, if you would prefer your group to design the mechanics of the clap on their own (highly recommended, as there are many successful designs), go for it!

The group will ready itself, and then on the count of "1, 2, 3," one huge collective clap will burst forth. Perfect for introducing a discussion about focus, goal setting and relationships.

Variations

- Each member of your group will help create one simultaneous clapping sensation by using their own hands.
- Once you have achieved the single clap (either method), shoot for two single claps in a row, i.e., clap clap!

MAGIC SHOES

A "get-your-group-from-here-to-there" initiative, involving more brains than brawn

AT A GLANCE
A group must move all of its members safely from here to there, using a magical pair of shoes that can only be worn once by each person and then only to move in one direction.

WHAT YOU NEED
A flat, open space
Minimum of 10 people
20 – 30 minutes

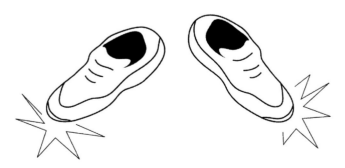

WHAT TO DO
Mark out two areas on the ground about ten metres (30 feet) apart. Although distance is not a critical factor, owing to the physical nature of this activity, anything beyond 10 metres (30 feet) gets tough.

Start your group on one side, and explain that their mission is to get from 'here' (pointing at the safe area they are standing in), across the 'poison peanut-butter' pit (or whatever you choose to concoct), to over 'there.' Other than their collective genius, all your group has at its disposal to solve this problem is an imaginary pair of 'magic shoes.'

Tell your group that it is not possible for anyone to enter safely into the 'peanut-butter' pit, lest they be swallowed whole. However, the 'magic shoes' will permit who ever is wearing them at the time to walk across the quagmire unharmed. But – and here's the catch – these shoes are so special, they can only be worn once by each person, and then only to move in one direction. Did you get that? Read it again. Also, to extinguish some of the more clever ideas out there, the shoes can only be worn by one person at a time, and they can not be thrown across the pit. That's it, go to it.

Typically, the solution will require many people to piggy-back one or two people across the pit. To this end, watch for unsteady crossings, or risky loads. Be prepared to stop any move that appears could "come a cropper" before it does. While involving a fair degree of physicality for some group members, this activity does allow the more cognitive members of a group to shine.

Variation

Assuming one person can only ever carry one other across the pit, how many pairs of 'magic shoes' (blessed with powers as described above) would be required to move everyone to safety?

EVERYBODY UP

A fantastic exercise to introduce the concept of group cooperation

AT A GLANCE
Starting in pairs and increasing in number to eventually involve the whole group, people attempt to raise themselves off the ground by leveraging the weight of their partner(s).

WHAT YOU NEED
A flat, open space, preferably with a non-slip surface
Minimum of 10 people
10 – 15 minutes

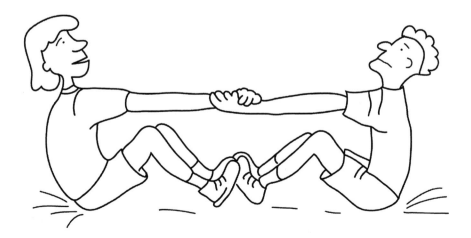

WHAT TO DO

Ask your group to separate into pairs, preferably seeking partners of approximately the same size. Each person sits facing their partner, the balls of their feet touching, knees bent and hands tightly grasped in front of them.

From this sitting position, each person will leverage the weight of their partner to pull themselves into an upright standing position. A little give and take will be required, and possibly several attempts to get it right. After a successful attempt, ask the partners to add another pair to their number and embark on a four-person assault, and then another, and then another and so on.

Something that begins as a simple cooperative stunt between two people soon becomes an initiative problem for the entire group as the configuration becomes more and more illogical and hilarious. If your group succeeds too quickly to raise itself, i.e., you're not quite ready to move on, or you believe not every idea was heard, suggest that the exercise be completed again but using a new technique.

Variation

Ask participants to sit back to back, and try to stand as a pair. With each success, add another twosome, etc. Beware, locking arms in this position may dislocate shoulders and should be approached with care.

POPSICLE PUSH-UP

A large-group problem calling for leadership, initiative and teamwork

AT A GLANCE

The entire group has to elevate itself off the ground for a period of 5 seconds with only their hands touching the ground.

WHAT YOU NEED

A flat, open space where people can place their hands on the ground comfortably
Minimum of 10 people
20 – 30 minutes

WHAT TO DO

Announce to your group that their goal is to elevate everyone off the ground for a period of, say, five seconds. Hands are the only part of their anatomy allowed to touch the ground. Furthermore, everyone must have physical contact with the group. End of story.

Likely, you will have to restate the problem several times, as people gasp at the images of handstands flashing by in their minds, or the fact that they can't use other objects to assist them (it's a people problem). There are many simple solutions to this fun initiative, so encourage your group to "think outside the square."

However, if you prefer, you may present the problem with a recognised solution, in an effort to spark people's imaginations. Start with one person

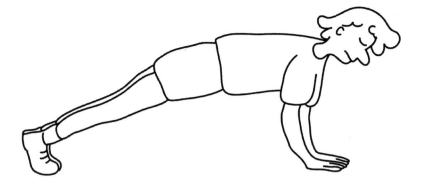

lying face down on the ground as if preparing to do a push-up. A second person lies face down at right angles to the first person so that the top of their feet are resting on the first person's shoulders. A third person repeats this procedure using the second person as their footrest, while a fourth person squeezes into this weave so as to connect everyone in a square. On "Go," everyone does a push-up. Ideally there should be four raised bodies, with only eight hands touching the ground.

Not all groups will succeed at the task, and that's okay. Look to process the experiences of working together as a team and developing problem-solving skills as an achievement.

Variations

- If you have a large group, separate them into smaller units. In this case, present the problem as "one problem – many work stations," whereby every unit is responsible for the success of the whole group. Typically, most groups will hear you say this, but they will almost immediately fall into the old "us versus them" routine. Makes for absorbing conversation during the debrief.
- Using any technique the group chooses, attempt to elevate as many people off the ground for as long as possible. Good luck.

THE CLOCK

Fast-paced initiative, that provides valuable insights into cooperation and goal setting

AT A GLANCE
Joined by hands in a circle, a group attempts to complete a sequence of moves – standing up, rotating a full 360 degrees one way and then the other and finally sitting back down – as quickly as possible.

WHAT YOU NEED
A flat, open space
Minimum of 10 people
A time-piece with a second hand
15 – 20 minutes

WHAT TO DO
Invite your group to form a circle, sitting on the floor. Each person should be close enough to hold onto their neighbour's hands. Hands held and sitting on the floor – this is called the "starting" and "finishing" positions. Now, rev your engines.

Explain to the group that on the call of an appropriate sounding signal, they are to stand up (holding hands at all times), rotate a full 360 degrees in a circle back to their original positions, then change direction and rotate back again to their original spots, and then stop and sit down together. Their goal is to complete this routine in the fastest possible time.

Provide your group with at least two attempts to set a nominal world record, and a third attempt if they choose, with several minutes for planning and discussion purposes. Ensure that people start and finish sitting on the ground, maintain their grip at all times, and are sensitive to whipping their slower colleagues around the circle at "breakneck" speed.

This is an awesome, albeit rather physical exercise for illustrating the power

of teamwork, and in particular, that a team is only as fast as its slowest member. Your processing may seek to relate these concepts to real-world situations, especially in terms of valuing people's diversity.

Variation

Challenge your group to beat a specific time (a target) that you set. On average, it takes about one second per person (plus a couple for safe measure) to complete the required moves.

SPAN THE ROOM

An initiative that sparks wild inventiveness and cooperation

AT A GLANCE
A group must create a total physical connection as it spans the distance between the two points.

WHAT YOU NEED
A flat, open space where people can lie and sit on the ground comfortably
Minimum of 10 people
20 – 30 minutes

WHAT TO DO
Locate a spot between two points where you can allow people to comfortably fill the gap and not impede traffic, such as two trees, the walls of a room or two fence posts.

This is one of those gradually-get-harder type of activities, so always pitch the first scenario at the lower end of the challenge scale. Focusing on your

chosen two points, instruct your group to use their bodies to span, or bridge the gap so that a continuous physical link is formed from one to the other.

In all cases, any part of one's anatomy can press up against the two end points, and the span need only occur for about five seconds. However, it's never as simple as just lying on tummies end to end. There's more.

For each challenge you will prescribe what anatomical parts can and cannot touch the ground. You will need to design each challenge specifically for the number of people you have in your group. For example, if you have ten people, and a distance of six metres (20 feet) to span, the parameters of using only five feet, two hands, two butts and a stomach would be doable. Yet, with three more or less people in the group, you will need to adjust the number and type of permissible parts.

As the group becomes more inventive, throw in a few curve balls, such as an elbow, a knee and a nose. In the beginning, you'll never know what your group can achieve which is why it's a good idea to start slow and easy.

After several progressively challenging rounds, chat about what it takes for a group to be inventive. What conditions are necessary to nurture creativity, and did the group manage all of its ideas?

Variation

Challenge your group to use as many different parts of their anatomy to touch the ground and the ends of the span, e.g., score a point each time a different body part is used.

FOUR POINTER

A monstrous activity that will mentally and physically challenge your group

AT A GLANCE
Groups of seven people attempt to cross an area by maintaining a maximum of four points of simultaneous contact with the ground.

WHAT YOU NEED
A flat, open space
Minimum of 7 people
10 – 20 minutes

WHAT TO DO
Set up your space with a this-is-where-you-are, and a this-is-where-you-need-to-get-to, with something like 15 metres (approximately 50 feet) between the two. Then divide your group into small teams of seven people.

Starting from within one safe area, each group of seven needs to transport their clan from here to the other side, while only using four anatomical points of simultaneous contact with the ground. A point of contact can be a foot, a hand, an elbow, etc, but there can only be four parts touching the ground at any point in time. So, to connect with your practical intellect, imag-

ine a group with four feet already on the ground. To progress forward, one person will need to lift their foot, and perhaps allow another person to put their foot (or hand or whatever) down.

Take note, that one part of a natural solution is to hoist people onto shoulders and backs. This is okay provided the group can demonstrate a high degree of safety consciousness through-out the journey. Accordingly, one of your discussion points may be around the level of attention afforded to safety during the exercise, and by this I mean emotional as much as physical safety. Especially in the context that this activity is often done with several groups at the same time, a spirit of competition may cloud people's better judgements regarding safety.

Variation

This problem can be accomplished with varying contact combinations, e.g., groups of five people with only three points of contact.

DON'T TOUCH ME

A magnificent exercise in continuous improvement

AT A GLANCE
Two lines of people pass by a designated spot as part of their process to switch places as fast as possible.

WHAT YOU NEED
A flat, open space
Minimum of 10 people
A time piece with a second hand
20 – 30 minutes

WHAT TO DO
Split your group into two equal teams, and delineate two lines of "spots" where members of each team will stand. The two lines should face each other about six metres (approximately 20 feet) apart, with team members spaced about a metre or two (three to six feet) either side of their colleagues.

Mark a circle about the size of a car tyre directly between the two team lines.

Starting on their own spots, explain that the two teams are working together to record the fastest possible time to switch sides. In the process, however, each person must touch some part of their body inside the middle circle as they pass through. The body part of choice is typically a foot, but so as to not limit people's creativity, I always broaden the options in my briefing. Finally and most importantly, in order to record an official world's record, there can be absolutely no physical contact between team members at any point in the switching process, e.g., the greatest risk of this occurring is when people pass through the centre circle.

Within the first few minutes, require that your group make their first official attempt, which will serve as a benchmark of sorts. Then allow your group to take five to ten minutes to discuss and rehearse an improved strategy, before recording a second attempt. Grant a third and final attempt if the group so desires.

While teamwork and problem solving feature heavily in this task, the primary focus is on continuous improvement and quality control. Observe the manner in which decisions are made, how a group manages the balance between planning and action, and the "risks" people will take to record a fast time.

Variation

Form a circle of spots for everyone to stand on, with a small circle marked directly in the centre. Same deal as above, but this time each person is entitled to move to any spot in the circle that is roughly opposite them, i.e., they cannot move to the two spots either side of them. A good option if you have an uneven number of people in your group.

HUMAN KNOT

One of the classic problem-solving activities

AT A GLANCE
Starting in a circle, people extend their arms and grasp the hands of two other people, and keeping a tight hold, work together to untangle themselves.

WHAT YOU NEED
An open space
Minimum of 6 and no more than 15 people
15 – 30 minutes

WHAT TO DO
Form a tight circle with your group facing into the centre. Ask each person to extend one of his or her arms in front of them and grab the hand of another, preferably not of their closest neighbours. Repeat this process with the other arm, but this time grabbing the

hand of a different person.

Now, from this mess of arms and co-joined hands, your group's task is to untangle themselves, but without ever letting go of their partner's hands. It's a tough gig, but typically once a few people start to wriggle themselves free of the tangle, the knots become easier to unravel. You could expect to see one large circle of joined hands evolve, or perhaps two or more linked or un-linked circles.

On some occasions, however, it may be physically impossible to untangle everyone. In these circumstances, the group is entitled to apply a little "knot first aid" to their problem. That is, the group can identify just one linking of hands that can be temporarily released and re-connected in a new position.

This process is a wonderful opportunity to test the group's decision-making skills, not to mention their capacity to stick with the problem. If necessary, knot first-aid can be applied a second time.

The activity is a natural for teaching perspective, patience and effective problem-solving techniques. Upon completion, invite your group to reflect on how decisions were made, the different roles people played and how conflicts were resolved.

Variation

Although technically a prop, invite people to grab the end of an article of clothing, or short piece of rope, rather than a person's hand. Ideal for larger groups.

LAP CIRCLE

A simple exercise that proves the power of cooperation and that a chain is only as strong as its weakest link

AT A GLANCE
Standing in a tight circle facing the back of another person, people simultaneously sit down onto the lap of the person behind them.

WHAT YOU NEED
A flat open space
Minimum of 10 laps
5 – 10 minutes

WHAT TO DO
Invite people to bunch in very closely to each other, so that they are facing to their left, and consequently at the back of the person in front of them. Then ask each person to place their hands onto the shoulders of the person in front of them.

You are almost ready, but for one last thing – it is critical that your group actually forms a circle – a round circle, not a box with a few corners. Look at the space inside the circle created by people's feet to get an idea for how round the circle really is.

Once the group is set, ask everyone to slowly bend at the knees and gently sit down onto the lap of the person behind them. Everyone is a sitter and a seat at the same time. When you have achieved a perfect circle, it's amazing how well supported the circle will feel. Throw your hands in the air and celebrate!

Okay, you are now ready to take the next step, literally. Moving one foot forward at a time – you may wish to chime

in with a "1, 2, 3 left, 1, 2, 3 right" if you choose – the group attempts to rotate its members a full 360 degrees around the circle.

Reflecting the true nature of a team, if just one person moves out of synch or moves slightly out of the circle, the whole group will collapse like a deck of cards. This can serve as a powerful example in your processing of the activity in relation to common goals, the impact of individual contributions and taking risks.

Variation

Instruct your group to walk backwards, or to move laterally toward an object five metres (16 feet) away.

SWEETS (DESSERTS)

There's always room for dessert at the end of a meal, no matter how full you are. And that's what this final activity chapter is all about.

In many cases, the games described in this section could have been classified as ice-breakers, warm-ups, tag games, trust exercises or group initiatives as already presented in this book. However, they stand out on their own because they are a collection of FUNN activities that scream an invitation to "play." These games have no finer purpose than to be enjoyed.

Beyond the pure, unadulterated pleasure of playing these games, you may uncover some inklings of intrinsic value – and your suspicions could be true, just don't tell anybody! Instead, approach these games with wild abandon, and then if you discern that they trigger more than just a fun time, explore the "what's happening here" with your group as you see fit.

Although they are tucked away at the end of the book, be tempted to indulge in these sweets at any time in your program. Indeed, I beseech you, because there is nothing worse than starting a program at 9 A.M. sharp yet finishing at 5 P.M. dull. Pepper your program with these games to energise and motivate your group to truly play and share, but most of all, to lubricate the wheels of your program's success from "Go" to "Whoa."

If you skipped the main meal to start with sweets, I suggest you take a quick look at the start of the Main Couse section before you dig in. I briefly describe what variables you can tweak to fit your activities to your group's needs. Also, I provide a short explanation of the format I have followed to describe the activities, which is equally applicable here.

Okay, time to play…

FUNN GAMES

These activities are played for the simple pleasure of having fun. They generate lots of good feelings, and can involve the whole group.

To squeeze the most out of your games, FUNN should also feature:

- Rules are kept to a minimum
- Elimination of players is avoided, or minimised
- Focus on play rather than competition

Just Games

Count Off
Four Up
Your Add
Slap Bang
Evolution
Pruie?
Categories Twist
Wink Murder

Circle Games

One Duck
King Frog
Antlers
Follow The Leader
If You Love Me Honey, Smile
Caught Ya Peekin'
The Rock
Ah So Ko
Have You Ever?
Commitment
Veggie Veggie
Wizz Bang

Audience Games

BF Skinner
The Story Game
Charade Line
What's The Key?
   The Man On The Moon
   Come to My Party
   Crossed or Uncrossed
   Dead or Alive
   Johnny Oops
   Surprise

COUNT OFF

Looking for a fun two-minute filler? This is it.

AT A GLANCE
A group attempts to count from 1 to 20 in one shot, where people at random say one number at a time, without establishing a pattern or speaking over another person.

WHAT YOU NEED
A comfortable, open space
Minimum of 5 people
2 – 5 minutes

WHAT TO DO
Invite your group to get comfortable wherever they are, and explain that you would like them to count to twenty. Sounds simple enough, but there are a few catches.

In an effort to count from one to twenty, an individual can only call out one number at a time, i.e., they can't call out two numbers in succession, but they can call another number later. Also, any time one or more people call out a number at the same time, the count goes back to zero. The biggest catch is that the group is not permitted to establish a pattern, nor is anyone allowed to indicate / gesture / motion to another that they should call the next number. The sequence of calls is purely determined by chance. That's what makes this game so contagiously fun.

The glee that strikes a group when two (or more) people speak at the same time after a long silence is what the game is all about. Within a few minutes, the group may not have reached twenty, but some spontaneous fun was had, and you successfully filled in a few moments.

Variations

• Ask your group to close their eyes during the activity.
• Choose any list to recite, such as the alphabet, the chemical tables, months of the year, and numbers of seven (e.g., 7, 14, 17, 21, 27, 28, etc).

FOUR UP

A silly stand-up and sit-down exercise

AT A GLANCE
Starting in a seated position, a group attempts to have exactly four people stand up for no longer than five seconds at any point in time.

WHAT YOU NEED
A comfortable, open space
Minimum of 8 and up to 12 people
2- 5 minutes

WHAT TO DO
Start with your group seated on the floor, or perhaps on chairs. You don't need a circle, but it's useful if everyone can see each other fairly well.

Explain to your group that you invite anyone to stand up whenever he or she wants to, but they cannot remain standing for longer than five seconds before they sit down again. The primary goal is to have exactly four people of the group standing up at any point in time.

That's it. The game normally lasts a couple of minutes – but what pandemonium and laughter is generated in that time! Truly ridiculous fun.

Variation
For larger groups, break into several sub-groups of about eight people, and play several games simultaneously. In my experience, the alternative of asking for more people to be standing doesn't work because any more than six people are hard to count quickly.

YOUR ADD

A great game for emphasising spontaneous interaction between people

AT A GLANCE
Two people face each other with their hands behind their backs, and on "Go," quickly reveal a pre-determined number of extended fingers to the other, while attempting to call out the sum.

WHAT YOU NEED
An open space for people to mingle
Minimum of 2 people
1 – 5 minutes

WHAT TO DO
Invite everyone to find a willing partner, and face them about a metre (40 inches) or more apart. To initiate a start to the game, one of the pair calls out "Set." At this juncture, each person places their hands behind their backs, and extends a certain number of fingers (that only they will know). Options vary between zero (both hands are clenched) to ten (all fingers and thumbs are extended).

When the second person is ready, he or she will call "Go." Together, each partner thrusts their hands forward with the chosen number of fingers extended. With all four hands visible, the first person to guess the total number of all fingers extended (for both players) is the champion. For example, if you extended six fingers and your partner shows three – the first person calling an answer of "nine" wins.

This game works best if people simply mingle about a space, and once someone spies a willing partner, they face off with them. This pair will engage in a couple of rounds, and at some point, move on to find a new rival, or more truthfully, someone less adept at mathematics!

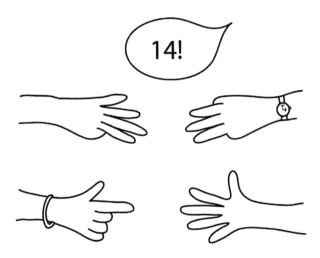

Variations

- Involve three or four players, each using one or two hands.
- The group calculates the sum of all the fingers other than those extended by the designated "subtracter" person, whose fingers you subtract from the sub-total. Similar applies with a person you identify as the "multiplier," where you multiply their number of extended fingers with the sub-total.

SLAP BANG

A more complex version of rock-scissors-paper, but just as much fun

AT A GLANCE
Two people face each other and perform one of a series of three arm- and hand-based movements to a shared beat, attempting to catch their partner off guard.

WHAT YOU NEED
An open space
Minimum of 2 people
5 – 10 minutes

WHAT TO DO
This activity was called the Henry-Robert game for years because it honoured the names of two campers from whom I first learned it! But they agree with me, in the absence of any other name, Slap Bang works pretty well.

Before we get into it, we need to establish two critical elements – a common beat and three distinct movements. The beat is as simple as slapping your thighs about once every second. And between beats, each person will assume one of three movements / gestures.

One move is to cross your arms on your chest (fingers touching shoulders) – this action is frequently called on because it keeps you "Safe." The second move called "Ready" is to clench your fists and poke your thumb up and over each shoulder, as if you were pointing with your thumbs at some thing behind you.

The third and deadliest move, called the "Bang," can only be used directly after the "Ready" move, and involves pointing your index finger forward and thumb up, pointing directly at your partner's tummy. Note, a person is not obliged to move into a "Bang" straight after producing a "Ready" move, but it is the only way a "Bang" can occur.

The object for each person is to catch their partner off guard by producing a "Bang" while the other is "Ready." If a "Bang" is created at the same time as a "Safe," then nothing happens, and the beat continues. A little hint for the slap-bang-savvy, if you see your partner move into a "Ready," be prepared for the possibility of a "Bang" at the next beat. Also, if two "Bangs" meet each other, they cancel each other out, and the beat continues.

Okay, once you've nailed these moves, here's how it all goes together. Ask everyone to find a partner who has a similar sized thumb, and stand facing them about a metre (40 inches) apart. Each person starts with a slap of their own thighs, and moves immediately into one of the three gestures, and then a slap, another gesture and so on. The slapping and gesticulation continues until a successful "Bang" is made.

For example, this is what a sequence could look like for me "slap-safe-slap-ready-slap-bang…," while my partner moves to the same beat with "slap-ready-slap-safe-slap-ready…" which means I earn a brownie point for scoring a "Bang" at the same time my partner was "Ready."

Variation

To adopt a less aggressive set of gestures, dispense with "Bang" and make it "Gotcha" with a simple pointing of one's index fingers only.

EVOLUTION

One of my all time favourite FUNN activities

AT A GLANCE
Physically portraying one of five distinct evolutionary creatures, a person attempts to win a quick game of rock-paper-scissors with other like creatures, to elevate their status and ultimately become a supreme being.

WHAT YOU NEED
A large, open space
Minimum of 15 people
10 – 15 minutes

WHAT TO DO
Feel free to spin whatever story you choose to introduce this game, the wilder the better. Here's my take on the evolutionary cycle.

Ask your group to help you create five evolutionary creatures. At the bottom of the food chain, we have the egg, followed by the chicken, then the dinosaur, then a Ninja Turtle (the ultimate human being), and finally, the all-knowing Supreme Being.

Each of these creatures has a unique physical representation. Invite your group to copy these movements and sounds as you show them. It's way fun, and besides, you look funny doing them on your own.

Egg – crouch down into a little ball with legs, and make muffled sounds.

Chicken – flap your arms by your sides and making clucking sounds.

Dinosaur – raise your arms above your head, take big heavy strides and make scary noises.

Ninja Turtle – make like a kung fu champion slicing the air with lots of karate chops and kicks.

Supreme Being – fold your arms like a genie, look calm and wise.

Now, explain that everyone will start the evolutionary cycle at the lowest level – the egg. To progress through the five phases, each creature must find another like-creature (not too hard in the beginning), and play a quick round of rock-paper-scissors. Whoever wins the round, steps up one evolutionary phase, and the "loser" will step down a phase. In the case of an egg, there is no lower phase, so if an egg loses a round, they just stay as an egg.

Everyone is aiming to become a Supreme Being, i.e., to do this, two ninja turtles must face off, and play a game of rock-paper-scissors – the winner becomes Supreme, and the loser returns to being a dinosaur. Once you become Supreme, you are no longer required to play (Supreme Beings are above all that), and they can simply stand out to the side with their arms crossed looking very self-righteous.

It's not possible to have everyone achieve Supreme Being status (nor is this desirable!), so plan to wrap the game up when you sense most people have had enough.

Variation

For a more continuous format, invite Supreme Beings to match wits with one another, i.e., play a game of rock-paper-scissors, and the winner remains supreme, but the loser goes back to being an egg!

PRUIE?

One of those games you just want to keep playing

AT A GLANCE
Mingling about a space with their eyes closed, people call out "Pruie?" to everyone they bump into, until they discover someone who does not reply, with whom they immediately link up and remain silent for the rest of the game.

WHAT YOU NEED
A large, flat space
Minimum of 15 people
5 – 10 minutes

WHAT TO DO
Hand out a set of blindfolds, or simply ask everyone to close their eyes for a few minutes. When darkness has descended, wander about your group and tap one person secretly on the shoulder. Explain to everyone that one person in the group has been tapped, and they will be the "Pruie" for this round. What's a "Pruie" you ask – I have no clue. It can be whatever you want it to be, but I do know it is a silent organism.

Next, instruct your group to get into "bumpers up" mode (hands up in front of chest, palms facing forward, elbows in) and wander about aimlessly within the immediate area. Each time they bump into someone, they ask, "Pruie?" as if enquiring whether this person is indeed the pruie. If the other person replies with " Pruie?", then they continue on. As you may have guessed, the only word that can ever be spoken in this game is " Pruie."

If upon making a "Pruie?" enquiry, there is no answer, that is the sign that this person is the Pruie, and the questioner should immediately latch onto them by linking arms in some way. From now on, that player has become a part of the Pruie, which means that if someone bumps into them, they remain silent too and so on the Pruie grows. Oh, and no matter who you are, everyone keeps their eyes closed.

Standing there in complete darkness, it is hilarious listening to those forlorn couple of folks at the end bleating out " Pruie?" The Pruie will find it hard to stifle their laughter, but should try to be as silent as possible. Game is over once everyone becomes a part of the Pruie. Be prepared to play another round or three.

Variation

For a large group, introduce 2 or 3 Pruies.

CATEGORIES TWIST

A simple, fun version of the standard Two Truths and a Lie

AT A GLANCE
Three people share two truths and one lie about three things that they have in common, and the rest of the group has to achieve consensus as to which is the lie.

WHAT YOU NEED
A comfortable, open space possibly with chairs
Minimum of 6 and up to 20 people
20 – 30 minutes

WHAT TO DO
People just love to find out stuff about other people's lives – even when it's not true! This activity just legitimises the whole process.

Divide your group into groups of three. Invite them to find a comfortable spot away from the rest of the group to share for about five to ten minutes as many categories their group has in common. There's always the standard "we all come from X town," or "we all brushed our teeth this morning", but encourage your groups to dig up some truly interesting, quirky stuff about themselves. For example, a group once proposed these three things "we have all seen a giraffe give birth at a zoo, we have all driven over 10 km in a car with the hand-brake on, and we can all sing the first verse to Eleanor Rigby by the Beatles." Wow, now that makes you think doesn't it?

Gather everyone back to the centre, and ask each group to state their three commonalities in as dead-pan a manner as possible. The object for all the other groups is to decide which one of the things is the lie. It's rarely easy, but always intriguing. You aim to reach consensus, but in most cases, you'll settle for a majority rule to keep things moving.

Variations

- Rather than present three things each person supposedly has in common, ask each group to simply present three facts (which are in fact all true) about the group, one for each person. The group has to decide which fact belongs to which person.
- Individually, a person presents two truths and one lie about themselves. The rest of the group attempts to uncover the lie.

WINK MURDER

A delightful way to die

AT A GLANCE
A secret "murderer" mingles about the group silently killing people with a deadly wink of the eye, while everyone greets one another and attempts to deduce who is responsible.

WHAT YOU NEED
A wide, open space
Minimum of 15 people
10 – 20 minutes

WHAT TO DO
Gather your group around you, and whisper to the huddle that "there is a murderer amongst us!" Amid the shock and horror of the news, describe that not even the murderer knows that they are the murderer... yet!

You can use whatever method you choose to secretly assign the "murderer," but here's a great "no props" technique I have enjoyed. Ask everyone to extend one of their arms with a thumb sticking up from their clenched fist into to the centre of the circle. With everyone looking out from the centre, you place your hand into the mess of thumbs and squeeze one of them once. You then instruct whoever belongs to that thumb to find another thumb in the group, and squeeze it twice. The person who has their thumb squoozed twice, is the murderer. Why do I suggest you go for the second squeeze – because it gives the leader a chance to be the murderer!

Now, explain to everyone that the

murderer's weapon of choice is a wink of the eye. Not a blink, not a twitch, but a fair-dinkum how-ya-going wink. At this point, you invite everyone to just mingle in the space provided, and simply greet each person with a smile and a look in the eye as often as possible. Two objects will now be hard at work – one, the murderer will be secretly winking away to "kill" everyone off, and two, everyone else will be hoping to catch the murderer "red-handed" and make an accusation to end their awful trade.

A few rules to add some order to this carnage:

- A person who has just been winked at by the murderer should wait at least five seconds before dying a histrionic death. The "dead' may lie in situ, or simply crawl off to the side.

- The murderer is not obliged to wink at everyone they greet. Indeed, I suggest this is a good strategy.

- If one of the living suspects who the murderer is, he or she may raise a hand and announce, "I accuse." At this point, the facilitator will halt proceedings and ask if there is a seconder. If there isn't, the game continues (but maybe not much longer for the accuser!!).

- If an accuser attracts the interest of a seconder, on the count of three (by the facilitator) each accuser must point directly to who they believe to be the murderer. If they each point at a different person, regardless if one of them is correct, they both die on the spot. If they both point at the wrong person, the same fate awaits them. Only if they both point at the murderer will the game end.

- No one may communicate or otherwise indicate to others who they believe could be the murderer.

This tragic tale will continue to play out until either everyone dies, or two people make a successful accusation. Play several rounds, randomly appointing a new murderer with each round.

Variations

- This time, everyone is obliged to shake hands with as many people as possible as they mingle. The murderer inflicts his / her fatal blow by gently rubbing or pressing their extended index finger into their soon-to-be victim's wrist as they shake hands. Naturally, the murderer may pass on their deadly hand-shake whenever he / she chooses.
- The murderer issues a "kiss of death" by subtly puckering up and almost blowing a kiss to those he or she wishes to kill. However, rather than dying, people swoon to their death with a giant exasperated sigh.
- Introduce the plague to any one of your choice of murders. Explain that as someone dies, they may collapse and happen to touch any one or more people around them, who in turn will catch the "plague" and die also. Suggest to people that they try hard not to spread the plague to the murderer – otherwise, it will make for a very, very long game.

ONE DUCK

Another one in a long line of hilarious it-should-be-so-easy-to-do activities

AT A GLANCE

Sitting in a circle, each person recites one part of a four-part phrase which multiplies each time it is completed, until the group has recited each part five times in a row without mistake.

WHAT YOU NEED

A comfortable, open space possibly with chairs
Minimum of 8 and up to 15 people
10 – 15 minutes

WHAT TO DO

Form your group into a circle and ask the participants to repeat the words "One duck – fell in – the pond – ker-plunk." The punctuation is deliberate, and should be reflected in the way you recite the verse the first time, i.e., it goes something like this "one duck" (pause) "fell in" (pause) "the pond" (pause) "kerplunk." Consider it a stanza comprised of four parts.

Instruct the group that you would now like them to repeat this verse – one person at a time in a clockwise direction – saying only one part at a time. For example, the first person will say "One duck," and the person to his / her left will then say "fell in," and so on.

Now for the tricky bit. When you get to "kerplunk," the verse is repeated again, but this time, each part of the stanza is said twice. So, the next person (i.e., fifth person in turn) says "One duck," followed by their neighbour repeating, "One duck," then passing to the next person who says "fell in," and the next repeats "fell in," etc, etc. Keep going, until you get to the "kerplunk" and "kerplunk" parts.

No prizes for guessing what happens next (I told you this was easy). The verse continues around the circle, this time with each part being repeated three times, then four times, and to achieve the all-time world's record, a climactic

fifth time!! One duck, one duck, one duck, one duck, one duck, fell in, fell in, fell in, and so on and on it goes. If your group can make it to this level, you all deserve a huge round of applause, or a long lie down!

Explosions of incredulous laughter will break out when someone, typically, forgets how many of which part of the verse has already been uttered. It seems so easy to count to five, yet after many failed world record attempts, I totally understand why the record is so elusive. Give it a go.

Variations

- Have the verse circle the group in the opposite direction.
- Make up your own little verse, with perhaps five, six or even seven parts.

KING FROG

A real winner, it is ranked somewhere in my top sixty activities.

AT A GLANCE
Sitting in a circle, a group performs a series of physical gestures and sounds representing animals to cause the King Frog or other player to make a mistake, bringing each person closer to the ultimate prize of becoming King Frog.

WHAT YOU NEED
A comfortable, open space possibly with chairs
Minimum of 8 and up to 20 people
20 – 30 minutes

WHAT TO DO
Everybody needs to be sitting down in a circle, positioned so that they can see everybody else from where they sit. The leader then invites each person to think of a unique action they can identify with an animal. For example, someone may choose to be a gorilla by beating their pumped up chest vigorously with their clenched fists, and making gorilla-like noises. Or flapping their arms like a bird and tweeting.

After a little thinking time, the leader starts off as King Frog or Queen Frog as the case may be. The action can be up to you, but try moving one palm (situated flat) quickly across the palm of your other hand to give the impression that the frog has jumped off his/her lily pad. Allow your group an opportunity to repeat your actions before continuing around the circle to learn all of the other actions, one at a time. Ensure that all actions are unique, i.e., you can have three types of birds, as long as they all have distinct gestures.

Explain that each round will start with King Frog. That person will perform the gesture, and then, perform the gesture of another animal in the group. This is a signal to this next "animal" that it is their turn. They must quickly do their action and follow it with the actions of another animal, and so on. A slow start

will help people get the idea of what is going on. Then the pace, and the fun, will pick up. But wait, there is more.

If someone is too slow, or mucks up the actions or performs them in the wrong sequence, everything stops. This person is obliged to leave their seat, and sit to the left of King Frog in the circle. This causes everyone sitting to the right of King Frog and this person, to move along one seat to fill the gaps. Now, get ready for the clincher –

the animal does not move with the person – the actions belong to the seat. So when a person sits in a new seat, they will assume the actions of a new animal. Oh, I can hear the groans from here!

The object of the game is to get into the royal throne, because then you have control. So, each time King Frog makes a mistake (that's a hint), everyone moves one seat to the left and closer to the throne. Hooray!

Variation

Exchange animal gestures and sounds with people's names. So, Jimmy starts with a "Jimmy-Jimmy, Jane-Jane," and then Jane replies with "Jane-Jane, Sanchez-Sanchez," and so on. If you wish, create a continuous beat of slaps (on laps) and claps, to guide the calling out of names, i.e., with each slap or clap, a name is called out.

ANTLERS

A perfect something to "fill-in" two minutes

AT A GLANCE
When signalled, a person will immediately place their outstretched hands to the sides of their head to create "antlers," causing their two neighbours to copy this motion with just the hand closest to them, before passing the signal on to another person in the group.

WHAT YOU NEED
An open space or a round table
Minimum of 8 people
2 – 5 minutes

WHAT TO DO
Start by forming a circle in which nearly everyone can see everyone else. Your group can be standing or sitting, and will work even around a dinner table while you wait for your meals to arrive!

You kick off by placing your open hands with outstretched fingers up to the sides of your head, thumbs poking at your temples. These are your "antlers," such that if someone were to look at you with blurry eyes from a distance, they could mistake you for a moose or a deer!

Now, explain that as soon as the "moose" produces its antlers, the two people on either side of them must immediately respond by copying the action, but only using that arm closest to the moose. That is, for example, the person to the left of the moose will only use their right hand to create an antler off to the side of their head. So, for every moose, there should only ever be four branches of "antles" or whatever the singular form of antlers is.

The antlered people can hold their position for as long as they like, but a quick game is a good game. So, at any time they choose, the "moose" only will bend their antlers forward on their head (keeping thumbs in position) while pointing with their two index fingers and looking to another person in the group. As you may have guessed already, this person becomes the next moose, who will immediately sprout

antlers alongside the two created by his or her neighbours. The old moose combo relinquishes their antlers, and the new moose continues the action.

You'll probably squeeze a good five or so minutes out of this silliness, which is all it is. Its raison d'être is observed simply in the hilarity generated when someone makes a mistake. There's no more serious consequence than a good laugh.

FOLLOW THE LEADER

A fantastic game to sharpen observation skills

AT A GLANCE
A person standing in the centre of a circle of people all moving in exactly the same manner, attempts to guess which one person is leading the changes in the group's movements.

WHAT YOU NEED
An open space
Minimum of 10 people
10 – 15 minutes

WHAT TO DO
An oldie but a goodie, particularly if you want to subtly develop focus and observation skills with your group.

Form a circle and explain that one person will soon be designated as "the leader" whose role is to initiate a series of movements which the rest of the group will copy. It is critical that the others follow the leader's movements exactly, and adopt any changes as soon as they become aware of them.

The trick is that the leader needs to remain a secret, because a second person who will volunteer to be the first "bunny" will not know who the leader is. Once nominated, the bunny will either leave the room, turn around, or close their eyes while the group nominates who will be their leader, i.e., this can be done silently by simply pointing at someone.

To start, the leader will begin a series of movements, such as walking on spot, or waving their arms a particular way. Then, the bunny will move into the centre of the circle and just look at everyone. The group will keep moving at all times, and secretly steal a glance at the leader (or other early-adopter) from time to time to pick up any changes in the movements. The leader should try to change their movements every ten seconds or so. Big moves are best and the most fun to watch.

Naturally, the circle people must be

careful not to make their glances at the leader too obvious too early. Once the bunny has guessed who the leader is, ask for a new person to volunteer to be the next bunny. Play several rounds.

Variations

- Invite the leader to become the next bunny after they have been discovered.
- If you have a high-performance group, ask the leader to be a "statue" moving from one frozen position to another. Hint: best time to move is when the bunny isn't looking.

IF YOU LOVE ME HONEY, SMILE

A sure-fire classic that can make even the most cheerless person smile

AT A GLANCE
One person, standing in the middle of a circle, makes an effort to encourage one of the seated participants to give up their seat by making them smile.

WHAT YOU NEED
A comfortable, open space possibly with chairs
Minimum of 10 honeys
20 – 30 minutes

WHAT TO DO
This game is best played when people are seated in a circle, either on the floor or in seats. People could stand, but they will invariably get tired and eventually submit to the ground anyway.
Whatever, it is important that everyone can see each other from where they sit / stand, so that they can comfortably witness the frolic that is about to unfold before them.

Everyone has a seat, except for you – you are standing in the middle of the circle. Your objective – as the only person without a seat – is to encourage anyone else sitting in the circle to give up their seat for you. And, you achieve this by encouraging them to smile after you have crooned the words "If you love me honey, smile." Now, a word of advice, you could demonstrate how this is done, but I recommend asking for a volunteer – it's much more fun watching a participant take on this role without being given any ideas as to how it should be done (because there is no way that it "should be done").

....will you smile for me?

In most cases, the un-seated person will slide up to some unsuspecting person in the circle, possibly sit on their lap, or play with their hair, swoon and so on and so on. If the seated person has not already broken out with a smirk or a smile, then it's time to apply the all-too-lethal and suitably "breathy" expression of "If you love me honey, smile". All of this can take anything from 10 to 30 seconds. Naturally, reasonable levels of decorum are expected of the smoocher – for most groups, you don't need to say this, but you be the judge.

If the seated person exposes a smile in the midst of all this romantic attention, they are asked to give up their seat for their "honey," and the next round begins – with this new person in the middle. However, if the seated person remains strong, and resists the urge to smile after the loving spiel has been given, they get to keep their seat, and the unseated (not to mention unloved) person moves on to approach a new person. Play for as long as you feel love is in the air.

Variation

Same set up, but this time the person in the middle is not permitted to touch anyone.

CAUGHT YA PEEKN'

A game about sneaking a peek at other people

AT A GLANCE
With their eyes closed, people steal a quick glance to see if they can catch another person whose eyes are open and attempt to call out this person's name to eliminate them from the game.

WHAT YOU NEED
A comfortable open space
Minimum of 10 peekers
5 – 10 minutes

WHAT TO DO
Invite people to create a circle (either seated or standing) in which everyone can see everyone else. Have the players close their eyes, and the game has started.

The object for each person now is to bravely open their eyes in an attempt to catch another person with their eyes open as well. Sometimes these two will spy each other at the same time, or one may catch the other looking in another direction. Either way, when a person observes another with their eyes open, they are entitled to call out loudly "caught ya peekin," and then call that person's name, e.g., "caught ya peekin, Jose." If two people spy each other at the same moment, whoever calls out first and correctly (remember, to be valid one must call the other person's name) wins the duel.

Of course, any time someone opens their eyes, they are vulnerable to

Caught you peekin Jess!

attack from another, and may have their name called out before they have a chance to call themselves. When a person is "got," I suggest they place their hands on top of their heads to make it clear to all those who are still "alive,"that they are out of the game, and are entitled to have their eyes open to enjoy the ongoing snitching!

By the way, note for your own interest how many people adopt the strategy to keep their eyes closed the whole time. It may be safe, but certainly not fun.

Variation

To encourage lots of peeking, grant each person three lives.

THE ROCK

A simple "guess who" type activity that takes "guts"

AT A GLANCE
Sitting in a circle, each person silently observes the overall behaviour of their colleagues as they attempt to guess who is secretly holding the "rock."

WHAT YOU NEED
A comfortable, open space
Minimum of 10 people
15 – 30 minutes

WHAT TO DO
I just love this activity, and so will your group once they understand what's going on. I picked it up in acting school, and after playing it for an hour every day for two weeks, got really good at it. It's very simple, but the connections and metaphors you may draw from this exercise to the process of your group's development are astonishing.

Start with your group standing in a circle, all facing into the centre. Ask them to close their eyes, and place both of their hands clenched behind their backs. Then, if they choose, each person may open one of their hands with palm cupped upward behind their back as if they might receive something in it. Only those who wish to receive the "rock" should have their hand in this ready-to-receive position.

Next, walk all the way around the outside of the circle, as quietly and steadily as possible, and place a small stone into one of the opened hands. That person will automatically clench their hand around the "rock," and then predictably start saying to themselves "oh wow...oh wow...oh wow...." You will often see a very visible change come over this person.

Once you have returned from whence you came, ask everyone to bring their clenched hands in front of them, open their eyes, and quietly and comfortably sit down with their hands visible to all. Remind people that they should sit in such a way that each person can easily

see everyone else.

Now the fun begins. Every person, even the one holding the rock, will appear to be looking, looking, all the time looking. Their task is to accurately guess who among their number has "got the rock." There is absolutely no talking, just looking and being open to what is so. Meanwhile, the rock-holder is spinning wheels inside to make it look like he or she doesn't have the rock, when in fact, everything about them is screaming "look over here!". It's an absolute classic.

Within 20 to 30 seconds, one or more people may raise their hands, and when called upon, point to and call the name of the person who they think is holding the rock. If they are correct, then congratulations are in order, and you may wish to enquire as to how they knew. But if the guess is wrong, the guesser is eliminated from the group and will push out of the circle, i.e., each person only gets once guess.

This activity teaches people to trust their "gut," or put in another way, they already "know" the answer – they just have to trust themselves to look and commit. If the connection within a group is real, then you can expect many people to quickly develop an ability to guess who is holding the rock. If the connection is developing, you will notice an increasing pace at which the group gets it. Otherwise, it just becomes a task of elimination.

Observe and note the "connection" that will be evident within the group at the end of the activity. Invite the group to enquire why this is so, and what impact this sense of the group can have on a group's performance.

Variations

- Use an alternative to the rock, such as a coin or a button, but something concealable.
- Same set-up, but invite the group to talk among themselves and attempt to reach "agreement" (naturally, it won't be unanimous!) within 2 – 3 minutes of sitting down.

AH SO KO

One of the best elimination games out there

AT A GLANCE
Sitting in a circle, people quickly adopt one of three consecutive gestures upon the signal of another in the group, and if they are too slow or apply the wrong gesture, they become a "heckler" to all those who continue to be in the game.

WHAT YOU NEED
A comfortable, open space
Minimum of 10 people
10 – 15 minutes

WHAT TO DO
Sit with your group in a circle, preferably on the floor, so that everyone can see everyone else with ease. Sometimes I like to be less than obvious, and may spin a yarn about the pre-language days of feudal China, before people realise that they are playing a game. Whatever, this awesome game is just asking to be wrapped in a story – here are the basics.

To set the scene, ask everyone to follow your lead and practice a few karate chops with their hands in the air. Then explain that one person will always start the game by placing one of their hands, palm facing toward the floor, directly below their chin, just short of their neck. Doing this in a kind of rhythmic, rapid motion, the person will utter an "Ah." Do it a few times, and invite everyone to practice it with you – the louder and more forceful the better.

Then, the person to whom the first player pointed at with their fingers (i.e., if they used their right hand to create "Ah," they will be pointing to their left neighbour) will add a guttural "So," and strike one of their hands, palm facing down, directly above their eyes (salute fashion). Again, practice this move with

your group, and ask people to note where they and their neighbours are pointing with the tips of the fingers.

The third and final gesture is assumed by the person to whom the second person pointed, who will extend their arm out in front of them pointing with their full open hand (held vertically) to anyone else in the circle. As they point, they will also look directly into the eyes of this person and call out a "Ko," which means "over there" according to my extensive research of the feudal Chinese language. The person to whom the third person points will start the whole sequence off again, by engaging in an "Ah."

To re-cap, by committing to their "Ah," a person always "points" to one of his or her neighbours who is responsible for delivering a "So," who effectively points to one of their neighbours, who then assumes the position of "Ko" who actually points to anyone else in the circle.

Now, here are the rules. The game always starts with "Ah," and will always follow the sequence of "Ah, So, Ko." When the group is aware that one of their number has made an error, there

is a brief interruption to the game. Everyone is invited to place their clenched fists into the centre of the circle, poke their thumb up, look directly at the person who made the mistake, and as they throw their clenched hand behind their back, call out loudly, "You're outta the game!".

Two things happen when someone is outta the game. One, they remove themselves from the circle, and the circle rejoins and the game starts from "Ah" within three seconds by the person to the left of the one who is out. Two, the player who is out, really isn't out – they actually have a very important job. In the best traditions of stand-up comedy, we invite all those people who go "out" to become hecklers. This means that they can do (almost) anything to put other people off their game, so that they too may make a mistake. Two things hecklers cannot do, however, is touch another person, or obstruct the view of any players. All other heckling is allowed.

It takes awhile to get there, but after a few dummy rounds, people get the hang of it really quickly, and will be eager to start. Game continues until

HAVE YOU EVER?

A wonderful energiser and get-to-know-you-better activity

AT A GLANCE

A person stands in the middle of a circle and asks a "Have you ever...?" question in an attempt to lure one or more people from the group who can answer "Yes" to leave their "spot."

WHAT YOU NEED

A large, open space
Minimum of 10 people
15 – 30 minutes

WHAT TO DO

Either standing on a "spot" (a shoe works well), or sitting in seats, ask your group to form a circle. One person, without a spot, will start in the centre of the circle – in the beginning, I like to be this person.

The mission for the person in the centre (the "questioner") is to encourage people to leave their seats, so that they may steal one for the next round. The way in which the "questioner" does this is by asking a question that is prefaced with "Have you ever....?". Fill in the blank with "been somewhere, done something, said something", but whatever the experience, it must apply to the questioner. So for example, I could ask "Have you ever stood at the lip of an active volcano?" because I have – Mt Ruapahu, New Zealand, just for the record! But I could not ask, "Have you ever given birth to a baby?" because I haven't. The "questioner" must be able to answer yes to their own question.

So, the "questioner" issues forth their enquiry, and usually, one or more people will be thinking "Yep, I've done that". Now, explain that everyone who thinks this is invited to leave the safety of their seat, and dart across the circle to find another empty seat. Of course, if seven people get up, there will be eight people looking for a seat, so someone will miss out, and this person will be the next "questioner."

It's a good idea to ask people to think of a question prior to getting caught in the centre saying, "Ummmm....". Also, encourage your group to think of questions a little more creative than "Have you ever brushed your teeth?" This will surely cause lots of movement, but there are plenty of questions out there that are a lot more fun and sometimes revealing, e.g., "Have you ever urinated in a swimming pool?" or "Have you ever stayed awake for more than 48 hours straight?". You will learn some amazing stuff about people, but remind your group that Challenge by Choice still reigns. A person may have actually done the thing that the "questioner" has asked, but if they do not feel comfortable "owning up to it," they do not have to move, let alone indicate that they had even contemplated it.

I like to honour those freaky folks who pose a question, only to discover that they are the only ones in the group who can respond with a yes. For example, ".. been hit by lightning?" and "... rolled an ambulance?" immediately come to mind. In these cases, I invite everyone to stand where they are, applaud for a few moments, and sit back down. Of course, the "questioner" must now think of another question.

If anyone gets stuck in the centre and can't think of a good question, or simply doesn't want to be there, ask for a volunteer to swap with them.

Variations

- Narrow the scope of your questions such as "Have you ever..... at school?", or "Have you ever..... with your friends?" This strategy will also prevent some groups from thinking up saucy questions when the gambit is very wide.
- Everyone has a "spot" and anyone can ask "Have you ever...?" at any time. In this case, everyone to whom the question applies is invited into the centre to join in a rousing chorus of – slap-slap (of thighs), clap-clap (of hands), click-click (of fingers), "yeaaahhhhh" (sung gloriously). They all return to their spots and another person gets up with their "Have you ever...?', and so on.

COMMITMENT

A fast-paced, frenetic activity

AT A GLANCE
Standing in a circle, two people choose to move quickly and secretly across the centre to swap "spots," whilst attempting to prevent the person standing in the centre from stealing their spot.

WHAT YOU NEED
A flat, open space
Minimum of 10 people
10 – 15 minutes

WHAT TO DO
For something completely different, start with your group in a circle, with each person standing on their "spot" (a shoe or chalk mark works fine).

Place yourself in the centre, and explain to the group that anyone at anytime is entitled to leave the shelter of their "spot" in an attempt to swap spots with another person on the other side of the circle. Typically, this commitment is initiated when two people eye each other from across the circle, give each other the nod to "go," and move with velocity to swap their respective spots.

When someone leaves a spot unoccupied, however, the person in the centre may choose to steal it. In this case, one of the parties who was in the process of moving spots will become the centre person. As you can imagine, you will need to alert your group to the possibility of collisions. I will sometimes add a further "rule" that says all moves must be accomplished without touching anyone in the process, in an effort to increase awareness of others.

The object is to see how many "swaps" one can make before losing their spot to the centre person. You can suggest to people that they count a point for every successful swap they make to compare notes later, or just play full out until everyone is pooped. In addition to being an excellent warm-up and energiser, this exercise is a great

introduction to a discussion about commitment – what worked, what didn't, what happened when intentions were thwarted, etc.

VEGGIE VEGGIE

A completely ridiculous, but totally delicious FUNN game

AT A GLANCE
Responding to the call of another person in the circle, people quickly say the name of their chosen vegetable and then the vegetable of another person, as if they had no teeth.

WHAT YOU NEED
A comfortable, open space
Minimum of 8 people
5 – 10 minutes

WHAT TO DO
Ever feel that you have trouble keeping your teeth in as you speak? Well this game has your name written all over it.

Move your group into the obligatory circle, and ask everyone to think of a vegetable, favourite or not. Everyone needs to nominate a different vegetable, so whip around the circle and invite everyone to announce their veggie. Any duplicates, simply request a quick change.

Now, explain that everyone left their teeth in the glass by the bed-side table this morning, causing them from now on to speak with their lips curled over their teeth. To start, one person will call out the name of their veggie twice, and then follow it up with the name of someone else's veggie. For example, it could sound like this "pumpkin-pumpkin, tomato-tomato" (it's kinda hard to type as if I didn't have my teeth in, but you get the idea).

Upon this start, the person whose chosen vegetable is tomato must now respond with their own veggie first, and then with the name of another person's veggie, and so on, e.g., "tomato-tomato, lettuce-lettuce", and then the lettuce-lover says "lettuce-lettuce, cucumber-cucumber," etc.

This is one of those fine examples of FUNN – if you see any intrinsic value here, let me know! Enjoy it for the pure pleasure it brings.

WIZZ BANG

A game with as many sounds as there are actions

AT A GLANCE
People quickly pass an imaginary object around the circle with a series of prescribed movements and sounds.

WHAT YOU NEED
An open space
Minimum of 10 people
5 – 10 minutes

WHAT TO DO
Announce to your group that you would like them to pass around an imaginary object, but there are only a limited number of ways in which it can be passed.

Start by setting up a circle, with people standing (preferred) within arm's reach of their neighbours. As part of the circle, you start by introducing a "wizz", which is demonstrated by flicking one's open hand as if shooing something away in front of them, and saying the word "wizz." Explain that there are only two directions a "wizz" can travel – to the left or right. To move the object to the right, one must wizz with their left hand, and vice versa.

When a person receives the wizzed object, they can choose to wizz it in the same direction, or introduce "bang" which effectively prevents the object from travelling any further in that direction, and causes it to travel in reverse. To "bang," a person will thrust their forearm directly in front of them, as if impeding the traffic of the object, and say, "Bang." Note: the correct arm to "bang" is the arm opposite the place from which the wizz travelled, or that which will have its palm facing the oncoming wizz.

Allow this action to settle in for a moment. Sounds of "wizz, wizz, wizz,

wizz, bang, wizz, wizz, bang, wizz, bang" etc. are what you can expect.

The options for sound and movement are endless, but here are two more sets of related gestures for you to try. Introduce one set at a time, and play until your group's interest is piqued.

Vroom – a person who receives the object may alter its path completely and send it anywhere in the circle, simply by looking at another person (the "Ahhhh" person) across the circle. A "vroom" is created by projecting the senders' arms and hands into the air as if guiding the flight of a dove released from one's hands, and of course, saying "vrooooommmm-mm."

Ahhhh – to receive, a person holds their arms up graciously as if being blessed by a higher being, and then retreating their arms to nurse the object gently into their chest. All of which compels the receiver to sigh heavily with an "ahhhhh," and then choose how to send the object on its way again.

Shoot – upon receiving the object, this person will hold it up as if it was a basketball, and "shoot," all the while looking in the direction of another person (the "Kerplunker") across the other side of the circle.

Kerplunk – the receiving end of the "shoot," this person forms a ring with their arms, and upon watching the object swish through, calls out, "Kerplunk." The object is now ready to travel again.

Variations

- Create your own methods of transportation, or invite the group to think of some zany ideas.
- Introduce two or more "objects" for the group to pass simultaneously.

BF SKINNER

A game that celebrates the discovery of specific kinds of human movements

AT A GLANCE

Two people work together in front of an appreciative audience to discover – through trial and error – an exact position and / or movement that the rest of the group had "created" before the pair entered the space.

WHAT YOU NEED

A comfortable, wide, open space
Minimum of 12 people
20 – 30 minutes

WHAT TO DO

In a moment, you will ask for two volunteers to leave the space, so that the rest of the group can work on a problem. There are no tricks up your sleeve, but you are well advised to explain everything to everyone before this pair departs.

The object for the two people who will soon leave the space, is to correctly demonstrate the exact position and / or movement of two people, as identified earlier by the rest of the group. For example, the group may choose to lay one person with their back to the ground and with their legs held up in the air by their partner. While the pair is absent from the space, the rest of the group will invite two others to display what the "desired position" looks like, so everyone has a very clear idea about what they want the unknowing pair to achieve.

When everyone is ready, invite the pair to enter the "performance area," and work by means of trial and error to achieve the desired position and / or movements. The group cannot speak to the pair, nor can they answer any ques-

tions. The only feedback the pair will receive from the group is their applause. When the pair "do" something that resembles one or more parts of the desired positions – for example, one of them suddenly lies on the ground – the group will increase the pace of their applause. It's a lot like the "getting warmer" game you played at school. The closer the pair get to the exact position, the warmer and more joyous the applause.

Most pairs will "get it" within five minutes. Beyond this, if there is a risk the pair will simply throw in the towel, feel free to offer a few hints such as what part of their bodies they could focus on moving. If the clapping is subdued, encourage the pair to do anything that is different from what they have been doing.

As facilitator, err on the side of "structural ease" when guiding your group to create the desired position. If it's too complex, with too many refined positions, the pair may never "get it," and that's no fun to anybody. Keep it simple.

Because truth is always obvious to those who know it, expect some classic moments of humour and side-splitting laughter from the audience as the unknowing pair struggle to find the "answer." And be sure that when they do, the group offers their most frenzied applause.

By the way, BF Skinner was well known for his study of human behaviour and movement. Does the name of the game make sense now?

Variation
Involve three or four people to create a position in which every person is physically connected in some way to the others.

THE STORY GAME

A terribly fun way to tell a story

AT A GLANCE
An individual attempts to recreate a story developed by the rest of the group without their knowledge, by simply asking "yes or no" questions.

WHAT YOU NEED
A comfortable, open space
Minimum of 8 people
10 – 20 minutes

WHAT TO DO
This game is so horrible, it's wonderful. Unlike many other games, there really is a trick to this one, and everyone knows about it except for one poor soul.

With everyone still bunched together, explain to your group that in a moment one person will leave the room, and while they are gone, the group will develop a short story that everyone needs to remember. The task for the individual who will volunteer to go first, is to recreate the story with a beginning, a middle and an end. And this person can only create the elements of the story by asking the group a series of questions that can only be answered with a "yes" or a "no."

At this point identify your "story teller," and then ask him or her to leave the space. Now, the thing we haven't said is that there is no story, but the "story-teller" doesn't know this. Explain that all your group has to do is agree on two "things" which will appear in the story which, in effect, the "story-teller" will make up. Also, one of these things must end with a vowel, and the other end with a consonant. For purposes of illustration, let's say the two things are "kangaroo" and "beer."

Now explain that when the story teller asks a question, any time it ends with a vowel, the answer is "yes" and when it ends with a consonant, the answer is "no." Simple and as tricky as that!

So, let the story begin. The story teller re-enters the space, and is told that to assist him or her in the creation of the story, there are two things that are featured – in this case – kangaroo and beer. The story teller launches into their first question, and with confidence that will fool the story teller into thinking that the group is very clear about their story, will receive an emphatic "yes" to every vowel-ending question and a resounding "no" on a consonant-ending question.

Oh, it's so cruel, but really it's not. Because, the delight that is exhibited on a story teller's face when he or she concocts the most absurd element to a story, and yet the group answers with a "yes" is priceless. "I-am-so-good-at-this" will be written all over his or her face. Of course, there are occasions when the facts don't seem to make sense, when a question is answered one way (because it ended in a vowel the first time), but is answered differently the next time (because it ended in a consonant). It's all part of the thrill of the chase.

As facilitator, be sure to keep the story moving, by encouraging the story teller to keep going over the facts of the story as they know it. Look for a beginning, a middle and an end. At some point, when it appears the story has reached a conclusion, support ample praise for a job well done. And then reveal the true story – there really was no story!

Variations

Invite two or more people to become the story tellers.

CHARADE LINE

Chinese whispers in the form of a mime

AT A GLANCE
With their backs to the "telling of a story," six people are invited, one person at a time, to see a short story being mimed to them, with the objective of passing the story along to the next person in line.

WHAT YOU NEED
A wide, open space
Minimum of 12 people
20 – 30 minutes

WHAT TO DO
Invite five people from your group to join you up front in the "performance area." Starting at the right-hand side of your space, ask them to form a straight line facing away from the centre, so each person faces the back of another person. Tap the first person's shoulder, and ask that person only to turn around and face you.

Their task is to observe closely everything that I (as story teller) am about to "perform," because very shortly, they will have to replicate this story exactly as they see it. The "story teller" cannot speak or use any verbal communication whatsoever, but simply mime their story.

As an example, I may mime the following – I walk in swinging a bag in my hand, I stop and pull out a chair and a fishing rod from the bag. I sit down, light up a cigarette, throw my line into the river, and start to relax. Suddenly, my fishing line starts to tug, and I feverishly try to reel it in. After much effort, I am disappointed to discover an old rubber boot off the end of my line. I empty the water out of the boot, put it on my foot, and walk off. End of story.

Other than the "audience," only the person I tapped will have been party to

my story. I now sit down, and this person taps the next person in line, and repeats the story exactly as they remember it, which on average is about 60% of what actually transpired, and 40% that never did. This process continues all the way down the line. As you can imagine, much like Chinese Whispers, the story is bound to get warped along the way.

During the re-telling of the story, the audience is permitted to laugh, but never indicate or say that the story is "wrong." They should simply sit back and enjoy – some of the most painful laughing fits I have ever experienced have been while watching this activity.

Once the last person observes the story re-told for the fifth time (in the eyes of the audience), most of the fun will be had. But it's worthwhile asking each person, starting from the very last person and working back along the line, what it is they "saw" happen in the story. The game completes with the person who first introduced the story performing it again, mostly for the benefit of those folks who had their backs turned away at the time it was first shown.

Variation

Invite two people to mime a story to another pair, the first in a line of I've-got-my-back-to-you pairs. You can provide some thinking time for the initial story tellers to develop their story. Or, to be held totally in suspense, allow the process to be improvised, so the initial story is created by the first story tellers spontaneously.

WHAT'S THE KEY

A lateral thinking exercise illustrating the concept that "truth is obvious to those who know it"

AT A GLANCE
An exercise is presented to a group of people, asking them to copy it exactly as it was shown to them. It's never what it seems to those who watch it.

WHAT YOU NEED
A comfortable, open space
Minimum of 8 people
5 – 15 minutes

WHAT TO DO
People always feel pretty smug when they "get" something, especially if there are others around them who haven't gotten it. Of course, everyone hates to be in the latter category. This next set of exercises are all about these experiences, but are shared with you to invite some fun into your program and perhaps demonstrate a few important learning outcomes (such as learning styles, perspective and lateral thinking), and not show that people are dumb.

These exercises all have one thing in common – the "key" is not what it seems to be. They are ideal for sparking a little lateral thinking in your group. People have to look beyond what is obvious, and discover another truth. As you can see, the connections one can draw from the experience of looking for the "key" to the real world are many.

Now, allow me to pass on a few words of advice about these types of exercises. First, do not present more than one or two in a row – seldom do the people who didn't get it the first time, get it the second time. Secondly, provide gradual clues to allow those who have not gotten it to get it. I will always tell people that "within five minutes everyone will have it, so keep trying." And thirdly, invite people to resist the temptation to whisper the answer to their fellow (frustrated) colleagues. This will only reinforce the fact that the latter couldn't do it without help, and getting it will not change their lives.

Variations

Here are just a few variations that illustrate a different form of the "key" in each case.

THE MAN IN THE MOON
Using your index finger, draw a circle in the air in front of you, and then add two eyes, a nose and a mouth. As you draw, you will first clear your throat and then say, "The man in the moon has two eyes, a nose and a mouth." You then invite some brave soul to repeat exactly what you did. Invariably, they will get it wrong. There will be all manner of attempts, many gallant, but they will all be missing the vital ingredient – the clearing of the throat at the beginning.

This is the "key." Unless a person clears his or her throat before commencing their recitation and drawing of the man in the moon, they will not pass muster.

COME TO MY PARTY
Ask your group to propose what "thing" they would like to bring to a party. In order to be invited, each person must bring the correct thing, such as a beer, an apple, or Darren. All of these "things" have something in common (the key) – two consecutive letters that are the same.

DEAD OR ALIVE
Point to a person in your group, and invite the group to predict whether they are dead or alive? If you say "Is (enter name) dead or alive?" the answer is always

dead, but if you ask the question any other way the answer is always "alive." Be sure to point to some people more than once, but change the question to bring back the dead.

CROSSED OR UNCROSSED

Sitting in a circle, use any two old sticks off the ground, and pass them to the person on your left and say "I pass these sticks to you crossed. How do you receive them?" No matter how you position the sticks as you pass them, or how the person receives them, the answer will always be related to how their legs are situated at the moment they pass the sticks. For example, the sticks I receive may in fact be crossed, but the answer will be "I receive them uncrossed" because at that time, my legs were uncrossed. A useful clue is to alter your legs mid way through your passing, and therefore, alter your passing statement, e.g., "I receive these sticks crossed (then you uncross your legs), and I pass them uncrossed."

JOHNNY OOPS

Use your index finger to touch each of the knuckles of your other hand, starting from the pinky saying "Johnny" with each touch. Then, after touching the index finger knuckle, sweep down the webbing between it and the thumb, and say, "Oops," then touch the end of your thumb and say "Johnny." Reversing your direction, sweep back down the webbing and say, "Oops" again, and 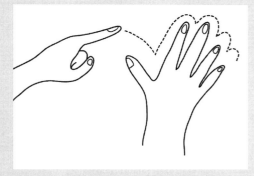 touch every finger knuckle with the word "Johnny." Finally look up and interlock your fingers together in front of you as they rest on your lap. Then, someone else gives it a go. The key here is what one does with their hands at the end of the exercise – everyone who interlocks their fingers together at the end gets it.

SURPRISE!

Sitting roughly in a circle (not critical), point your finger to anyone in the group and say "Surprise!". Extra style points are awarded if you elongate the word as you wag your finger about aimlessly, such as "Sssuuuuuuuurrr...", then sharply focus your finger on one person with a rousing "...prise!". After some moments have passed, ask your group to nominate whom you took by surprise. As you may have guessed, it has nothing to do with who is pointed at – it will always be the first person to speak after you have said the word "Surprise." To this end, it's a good idea to allow some time to elapse (and therefore provide a space for a number of people to speak up – they always do) before you reveal whom you surprised.

TEA & COFFEE

This section is designed to give you a few pointers about the many resources that Project Adventure can provide to help you derive the most out of your programs.

There are literally dozens of training workshops, books and resources out there designed to enhance the knowledge and activities you have gleaned from this publication. But, to be honest, the best way to learn this stuff is to do it. Get out there, have some fun, fail forwards and remain inventive. By attending one of our training workshops, you will not only get to see many of the activities described in this book played out for real, but also discover many invaluable networking opportunities.

It is Project Adventure's primary mission to help people use Adventure as a catalyst for personal and professional change and growth. Feel free to contact us at any time if you would like support as you introduce Adventure into your setting. We've been doing it for more than 30 years, and in almost every possible setting imaginable. Bring the Adventure home, and have fun!

PROGRAMMING PHILOSOPHIES

The discussion that follows aims to provide you – whether you are new or not-so-new to the programming field – with a few guiding philosophies designed to inspire successful programming.

The success of your program relies on many factors, and most of them are profoundly related to preparation. Your training as a program provider, the breadth and depth of your repertoire of activities, even the arrangement of logistics such as equipment, food, venue and transport (where necessary) are all important to your success. Yet, I would argue that the most critical factor to success is the preparation of your group.

The programming philosophies of Sequencing, Challenge by Choice, FUNN, the Full Value Contract and the Experiential Learning Cycle, are intended to support and promote the attributes of success in your program – risk-taking, fun, challenge and safety (both emotional and physical). Or in other words, they are designed to invite your group to play, trust and learn.

These five philosophies inspire all of the activities in this book, indeed, pretty much all of Project Adventure's curriculum. Work hard to keep them in focus and in play at all times.

SEQUENCING
The right activity at the right time

While there is no magic formula that can help achieve the perfect program, often a critical ingredient to achieving success is the sequence of your program's activities.

Sequencing involves making the order

of your activities appropriate to the needs of your group. This means preparing your group, both physically and emotionally, for what's coming up. Did you get that? Preparation; sequencing is all about preparing your group for the challenges that lie ahead. This is not a new concept, but one that applies across the board regardless of content.

The use of "lead-up" activities is crucial. Without appropriate lead-up, you may jump into activities for which your group is not ready. For example, the use of a few introductory or "ice-breaker" activities, which help people to get to know one another and allow them to "let off some steam," may assist you to create a more exciting and energetic start to your program. Or perhaps, these activities could highlight a particular learning outcome or skill which you will want to call on later.

Sequencing also relates to the necessary adjustments that are made to your program as you progress – activity by activity. Because all activities elicit a range of behaviours, feelings and attitudes – and no two groups are the same – your own observations of what is going on with a specific group is an equally important key to sequencing.

For example, just because you've played "Gotcha" a dozen times, and most groups you work with exhibit similar characteristics, does not mean that each group should not be treated individually. It also means that even though the agenda says that your group is supposed to be doing a certain activity at a certain time, if they are not ready, don't push them. Change what you had originally planned to do, or get to it after you've added a few more preparatory activities.

It's like "learning to crawl before you walk." Appropriate sequencing will lead your group to success, but it will also help you create a fun, positive experience in which everyone feels valued, rather than pushed.

Here's a simple model of sequencing that I've found useful over the years.

Ice-breakers. Activities that provide opportunities for your group to "get to know one another," have fun and begin to feel more comfortable with each other. Initially, you can expect this stage of the program to be success-oriented, with an emphasis on fun, high interaction and minimal decision-making skills.

De-inhibitizers. Activities that encourage people to assume more risks – emotional and physical – and extend their comfort zone. Warm-ups, tag games and trust exercises are good examples. Emphasis is on trying (rather than success / failure), having fun and creating a positive atmosphere in which the group can begin to feel supported and more confident.

Skill Development. At this stage, your group possesses the requisite skills to communicate, cooperate and trust one another within a safe, supportive environment. They are now prepared for the "main event" to develop whatever you had in mind. This can range from developing skills in a basketball clinic, to developing social skills within the framework of a series of problem-solving activities, to creating a sense of play / performance for a high-energy, fun evening program to conclude a three-day school camp.

Ask the question – what skills are you trying to develop within your group and / or program? i.e., is it fun, recreation, social skills, sporting prowess, etc. Then, think about how you can best prepare your group to meet this challenge, and achieve success.

Where are the trust activities?

When I first started out, I believed that "trust" activities were a necessary, yet separate stage of this sequencing model, i.e., somewhere after de-inhibitizers but before the big development stuff. But, I've grown up now, and this view just doesn't fit anymore.

As my understanding of programming has developed, I realised that trust was something I fostered right from the get-go, as soon as I said, "Hi, my name is Mark." Sure, there are specific trust exercises (like Funny Walk, Trust Fall, etc) that are devoted to the development of trust, and owing to their nature, are properly conducted later rather than sooner in a program's sequence. But, the earliest signs of trust are born in the cacophony of laughter and smiles you generate in your first lead-up activities, maybe even in your introduction.

Trust is gradually developed as your sequence of activities progress. It starts small, and builds so that by the time you are about to embark on the biggest parts of your program – probably the very reason they are together, to develop a particular set of skills perchance – you have the necessary levels of trust in place to achieve a successful (i.e., desired) outcome.

How does one measure trust anyway? You can't, you kinda just get a feel for things, a sense of the "I-feel-safe" factor, so to speak. And that's why it is so important to constantly observe the interactions and reactions of your group, and make necessary adjustments (to the way you say things and plan and present activities) as you go. And like most things, the more you deliver, the better you get at judging the fluctuating levels of trust, needs and skills of your group.

Picking the right activity

There are a number of tools "out there" which aim to assist you read or assess a group's needs at any given time in your program. To help me select the right activity at the right time, I can think of no better instrument than GRABBSS. Regard it as your "grab bag" of clues which can help you juggle the plethora of activities you have in mind and determine which one is "right" for now.

GRABBSS is a series of questions divided across seven key modalities, that is, elements you can observe and evaluate about your group, and the impact your program is having on its development. One element is not necessarily more important than another, but the acronym reads as follows:

Goals How does this activity relate to the goals of the group and overall program, or those that you see emerging? Basically, this element is asking, why are you doing the activity?

Readiness Is the group ready (emotionally and / or physically) to do the activity? What needs to change before the group has the ability to undertake the next stage of the program?

Affect What is the feeling of the group? What sensations are they experiencing – boredom, excitement, apathy, resistance, etc?

Behaviour How is the group or individuals acting? Are the interactions between members positive or negative for the group? How cooperative are they? Will their behaviour be appropriate for the activity?

Body What are the physical abilities of the group? What physical characteristics of the group will impact on the program? Are they tired, do they substance abuse, do any individuals have a disability, are they hot or cold, etc?

Stage What stage of development is the group in? Using Bruce Tuckman's popular rhyming schema to describe the varying levels, are they forming, storming, norming, performing or transforming? Does the group need additional skills to function at a higher level (stage) of development? Generally speaking, the higher the level of group development, the more challenging you can design your activities.

Setting What is the physical setting of the program, and the "cultural" background of the participants? Are you inside or outside, secluded or likely to be disturbed? Is the space limited? How long have the people known / worked with each other?

In essence, you are constantly asking yourself these types of questions to help you make an informed decision about what is appropriate for the "what's next?", i.e., what does my group need next?

For example, you may be working with a school group for the purposes of developing team and communication skills. Even though your agenda suggests that you should do X activity at Y time, if the group has not demonstrated that it has the skills necessary to succeed (i.e., the group is not ready), then you are well advised to alter your program sequence. Add one or more alternative activities that matches the skills of the group and aims to develop their readiness for the desired activity.

Or, perhaps the group is ready to move onto the next more challenging activity, but "cooled" down significantly during the processing chat – throw in a quick "warm-up" to move their bodies once again before moving on.

Now, it would be nice if for every answer you came up with for each of the elements of GRABBSS you could assign a number, and then just calculate the sum of all these numbers, and this was the pointer to what activity to use next. Yes, it would be nice, but totally implausible. Rather, GRABBSS is about observing your group and planning on the run – all of the time. It is a constant asking, what does my group need to achieve success?

For a more elaborate description of GRABBSS, check out *Exploring Islands of Healing* by Jim Schoel and Richard Maizell.

CHALLENGE BY CHOICE
Empowering through choice

This means you give the participants a realm of choice to determine their level of involvement (or challenge) in a given activity. Nobody is forced to do anything they don't want to do. The motivation to participate comes from within, rather than from external influences.

A choice not to participate in a particular activity, or (more often) to assume a role that is more comfortable for the participant, is always respected. Real success and learning occurs only when individuals choose and commit to their own standards and goals that are personally meaningful.

However, operating within the programmatic context of Challenge by Choice is more than simply allowing your participants to say, "No" and pull out of an activity. It's about creating a safe learning environment for your participants which invites them to make appropriate decisions in an atmosphere they expect will support them. In essence, you aim to empower them to make their own decisions, but also encourage them to "give it a go."

As a program facilitator, you have to be profoundly related to this concept of choice, especially in relation to your program design, and your language. It's one thing to say "...this program operates under the philosophy of Challenge by Choice...". But it's entirely another thing to be responsible for a program which speaks to, honours and fosters an atmosphere in which people genuinely feel comfortable to make decisions regarding the level of their participation.

Creating a "safe" learning environment (in both the physical and emotional

senses of the word) should be your primary concern. A program in which people feel safe to express themselves, and experience the freedom to make their own decisions will produce an extraordinary environment in which play, trust and learning can occur and flourish. Challenge by Choice is one of the most important tools you can employ to help you develop this atmosphere.

A word on participation

Many people – facilitators and participants alike – often confuse Challenge by Choice with "participation." This is a simple trap, but people can participate in so many different ways, it's more than just running around.

A case in point. I was involved in the delivery of a pilot program which integrated police recruits and, for the want of a better word, "street kids." To be honest, I would be hard-stretched to think of two more diametrically opposed groups. Anyway, our first morning was humming along, but two of the street kids chose not to join in. Challenge by Choice had been introduced, so I respected their decisions to sit out. However, I did take it personally, that even despite a full-out-fun program, my encouragement and the urging of their friends to join in (i.e., "it's really cool"), I could not motivate these two girls to participate. By day's end,

the two girls did not move from their comfortable sidelined position. Sigh....

And then, it happened. To wrap up the day, the top brass of the police squadron asked the group a few questions, a debrief of sorts, including the old standard "...what did you learn about each other today?" To my shock, one of the two girls put up her hand. I'm thinking, "What entitles you to answer this question – you didn't participate all day?" She replied something to the effect of "I didn't think the coppers would laugh at the same things we did!" And then it hit me.

This girl had been participating all day, she just chose (for whatever reasons) to do it from the sidelines. It was one of those "ah-ha" moments we all strive for, and was only made possible because of the atmosphere that had been developed during the day, particularly enabled by the use of Challenge by Choice. If this girl had been forced to participate, I am certain the result would have been very different.

The choice not to do an activity can be just as powerful as the choice to do it – in all cases, the choice – if it is made freely and in an atmosphere of support – will empower the individual. When viewed in this context, Challenge by Choice becomes a challenge of choice.

FUNN

Fun is okay, or people learn more if they are having fun

Obvious fun is very hard to stand away from, and so the FUNN – a whimsical acronym for Functional Understanding Not Necessary – element of a program goes a long way towards involving everyone's participation. Karl Rohnke,

author of many Project Adventure titles, coined this term many years ago, and it's an absolute gem. Applied liberally throughout your program, it says "if it's fun, I want to be a part of it."

FUNN means that it's okay to be involved in an activity for no other reason than to enjoy it. You, or your participants, do not need to have a special reason to do an activity. Do it for the laughs, the play and the good feelings it creates. You will be surprised by the results. As I described earlier in this chapter, we should take fun more seriously!

On the face of it, having fun during the course of a "serious program" can appear to some people (dare I say, many decision makers) as folly; a serious waste of time and resources. Or, in other words, "Why are we playing childish games when we should be ... (feel free to add whatever serious intent you care to name here)?" This school of thought would have us believe that playing and learning is tantamount to throwing a bucket of dollar bills into the wind, and trying to catch as many of them as you can with oven mitts. You can't be serious, and I rejoin – that's exactly the point.

It is absolutely essential to inject a heavy dose of FUNN style activities into your program for, ironically, lots of valid, intrinsic reasons. I can not stress this enough. Programmatically, there are mondo motives for adding FUNN to your program – to invite people to laugh, to share, to play, loosen up, set the tone, or to change the pace, etc – all of which contribute manifestly to the development of trust. Full stop. Yes, FUNN is good, agreeable, contagious, its own reward, etc, etc. But it will also help facilitate your program goals – the beauty is, your participants don't need to understand that this is what's happening. It just goes on around them.

I often remark that "if in the midst of having an outrageous time today, you should stop and ask yourself 'why are we doing this?', I suggest that you don't work too hard to find an answer – simply enjoy it for what it is". You see, I want the budding trust to sneak up on them. They'll see it as just having fun, but I know better. The old "you-have-to-trust-each-other" while I wag my finger trick just doesn't work. Oh, and it's no fun either. Injecting FUNN into your program will give your participants the permission they crave to play – truly play – and happily for you, the motivation to generate a safe place, which inspires good sharing – which leads to trust – which can stimulate learning. Voila!

EXPERIENTIAL LEARNING CYCLE

Learner driven learning

The Experiential Learning Cycle is the foundation of all experiential or Adventure-based programs. It suggests that the transfer of learning will be more effective if what is being learned is discovered though actual experience. Or, as it is sometimes referred to, as "learning by doing."

Processing the Learning Experience

You may have heard the phrase "let the mountains speak for themselves." It suggests that anything that your group may learn from an experience will happen of its own accord. Happily, this philosophy may work for those who heard the message. But what about those who didn't hear a message, or perhaps, heard the wrong message? They risk leaving your program without gaining any value from it, or worse, receiving a negative experience.

Clearly, the practice of simply "doing" does not in and of itself create "learning." If your goal is to invite your group to have fun, then this "hands-off" approach may be fine. But, if you are looking to have an impact on learning, you may need to "facilitate" this process. Indeed, the process of reflecting upon an experience in order to gain meaning, and then connecting these meanings to "real life" will provide many opportunities for learning. This process has been captured by David Kolb in four interrelated phases of what he refers to as the Experiential Learning Cycle.

This process (also referred to as a debrief, or review) provides an opportunity for members of your group to come forth with their own perceptions of "what it all means." Guided by your questions, participants can talk things out and tackle relevant issues, such as communication and leadership within the group. And, within the context of a safe and supportive atmosphere, they

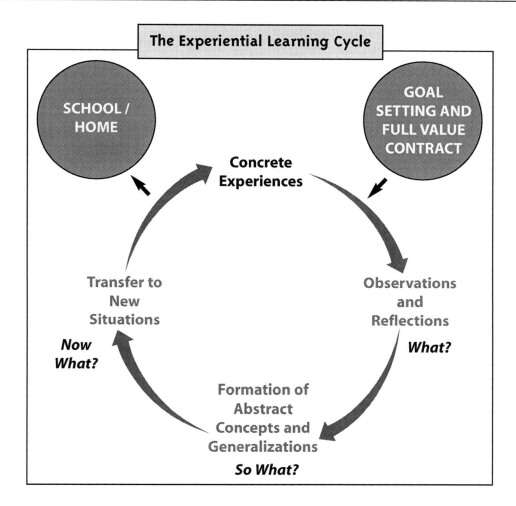

The Experiential Learning Cycle

SCHOOL / HOME

GOAL SETTING AND FULL VALUE CONTRACT

Concrete Experiences

Transfer to New Situations

Now What?

Observations and Reflections

What?

Formation of Abstract Concepts and Generalizations

So What?

can also provide feedback to one another and raise significant learning points.

Anecdotal evidence (i.e., lots of people tell me) suggests that many program leaders have difficulty with the processing or debriefing elements of an activity. We worry that we won't be good at it, or our group will resist talking about stuff, or put simply, the pressure of trawling for pearls of wisdom every time makes it all too hard. Well, relax. Volumes have been written about

the art and science of processing, and they pretty much all boil down to three simple steps.

What, So What, Now What?

Just as the activities in your program need to be sequenced carefully, you should also sequence your processing discussion.

1. **What?** Reflecting on the details of "what happened" in the experience(s).

2. **So What?** Generalising these facts, making connections and looking for patterns.

3. **Now What?** Applying this information to the next activity, or ultimately, to people's real lives – at school, home, work and play.

Ease into your debrief by beginning with the facts. Ask "What?" type questions to start with. This will get your group talking, and to be honest, this is the hardest part. Some examples may include, "What did the group do next when the second beach ball was introduced?", "What methods were used by the group to solve the problem?" and "How did the group come to a decision?"

Then, if appropriate, you can move the discussion to the next step – interpreting or adding meaning to what happened. The "So What?" step presupposes that we do something with what we hear, to find out what this all means, and perhaps make generalisations. "When groups are in discussion, it is best for one person to speak at a time" is a good example of a generalisation at work.

At this point it is important to ask questions that help the group find its own answers. This is a good place in which to address issues such as trust, communication, safety, leadership and cooperation. These "So what?" type of questions may look like "What made the method of solving this problem so effective?", "Why did the group become frustrated?" or "How did it feel to be left out of the decision making process?"

The most powerful step is moving the group on to consider the "Now What?". A standard question to ask is "What have we learned in this activity that we can apply to …. (whatever the reality is for this group)?". Sometimes, these connections are very clear, while other times the group has no idea. Again, this is where you come in.

Use questions that help your participants see the big picture, such as, "Give me an example of how we could improve our cooperation based on what we have learned from this activity" or "What will we do differently as a group next time?" and "What goals can we set for this group to improve your overall performance?".

Do not expect to see the blinding light every time you sit down with a group to discuss what's happened. But, if you are keen to draw more than a fun time out of your program, provide a structured reflection period from time to time. It will not only supply you with tons of valuable information about how your group is travelling, but will expand your group's learning opportunities.

FULL VALUE CONTRACT

Agreeing on how we are going to look after ourselves

Creating a safe, supportive and fun atmosphere has got to be one of the most important responsibilities of a program provider. To not focus on this critical task, is akin to driving without a seat-belt – no matter how short or long the drive, there is always the chance of an accident.

The Full Value Contract is a bit like a seat-belt. It is an agreement (a device) that helps individuals and groups achieve their goals in a safe and supportive learning environment. No matter what group or program you care to mention – from your standard weekly two-hour basketball clinic to multi-day, residential Adventure programs – every one of them will benefit from the process of consciously defining what is expected of people's behaviours.

The Full Value Contract – in its many and varied forms – is the cornerstone of Project Adventure's work. With Full Value, you can establish workable group "norms" (that is, accepted ways of being) that foster and manage appropriate behaviours. And it's always "appropriate behaviours" for this group, right here, right now. Every group is necessarily different. In theory, you may expect values such as "to be honest" or "respect for everyone" to be common across the board, but, in practice, the understanding of these concepts may vary widely.

What the Full Value Contract looks like

Basically, the Full Value Contract or agreement is a statement (either written or oral) made by each member concerning their shared values and how they wish to be treated. Values such as respect, openness, acceptance of differences and patience are time-honoured contributions. "No put-downs," "alcohol-free," "constructive feedback" and "everyone has an equal say" may be examples of more specific agreements for specific populations.

Importantly, the Full Value Contract ought to fit the unique goals, characteristics and sprit of your group. No matter what shape it may take, it is a shared creation, and should embrace three broad tasks:

1. To understand and create safe behavioural norms under which the group will operate;

2. Seek a commitment to adhere to these norms by everyone in the group; and

3. To accept a shared responsibility for the maintenance of the group.

Importantly, the inspiration for and the shape of whatever agreement is formed must reflect the needs and characteristics of your group and program design. The Full Value Contract you develop for a one-hour class with students will differ significantly to that created for a residential therapy group. So will the agreement formed between adjudicated youth and that developed for a one-day corporate training workshop.

Here are just three ideas regarding alternative designs:

Play Fair, Play Safe, Play Hard. Introduced "as is" at the start of your program, perfect for short programs, and young people.

Be Here, Be Safe, Be Honest, Commit to Goals, Let Go & Move On, Care for Self & Others. Presented within a discussion of the six components, ideal for older youth and adults, and programs of a longer duration.

Do-It-Yourself. A creative means, by which you invite the group to come up with their own tenets of agreement – suitable for most ages. It may be written down (or drawn) or communicated verbally.

Keep in mind, and continuing the analogy of a seat-belt, consider the Full Value Contract as a fluid and continuous process. Sometimes, the seat belt may have to be really tight (for example, asking people to sign a written document which explicitly prescribes the agreement), or quite loose to allow some freedom of movement (where the group may alter the framework of the agreement as their skills develop).

Why bother?

I can't tell you the number of times I have had a group explain to me that they don't need a "full value thingee" because "we all get along great." These are the groups I worry about the most.

Yeah, sure, there are some rare groups that really do care for one another, and echo a wonderfully safe and supportive environment in which to play and learn. But most groups, no matter the reason for their existence or length of program, will benefit from some form of shared, conscious agreement that governs their behaviour. Even groups that have been together for a long time – such as a school class, or a work-team – will gain a lot from the process of sharing and making conscious those aspects of their collective norms that are acceptable, and those that are not.

In my experience, much of the discussion reflects typically unwritten, unspoken laws of "how we do things around here." Naturally, for those groups that are just forming, there is no such thing. Hence, even if the list of "norms" is exactly the same for every member of the group, the process of actually sharing and making this agreement conscious is whole-heartedly beneficial.

Once it has been formed, a Full Value Contract presumes specific expectations for all group members, i.e., everyone knows where they stand. And then its full power may come to bear, because it transforms into a self-monitoring / policing agreement. Responsibility for the growth and safety of the group no longer rests solely with "the leader." If something is amiss, the Full Value Contract gives any individual permission to bring it to the attention of the group, and request that it be addressed.

PROJECT ADVENTURE BOOKS AND PUBLICATIONS

Project Adventure has been publishing books and materials for the field of Adventure Education since 1974. Our titles cover all aspects of Adventure – from games and initiatives to Challenge Ropes Course use, from program safety to theory and practice. Some of our most popular titles include:

The Guide for Challenge Course Operations by Bob Ryan

Physical Education Curriculum – Elementary, Middle & High Schools by Jane Panicucci, Alison Reingold, Amy Kohut, Nancy Stratton and Lisa Faulkingham-Hunt

Exploring Islands of Healing by Jim Schoel and Richard Maizell

Silver Bullets by Karl Rohnke

Quick Silver by Karl Rohnke and Steve Butler

Backpocket Adventures by Karl Rohnke and Jim Grout

Gold Nuggets: Readings for Experiential Education edited by Jim Schoel and Mike Stratton

Islands of Healing by Jim Schoel, Dick Prouty and Paul Radcliffe

Cowstails & Cobras II by Karl Rohnke

ADVENTURE ACCESSORIES

Adventure programs, both with and without a Challenge Ropes Course, need accessories that can often be difficult to find or adapt. The Project Adventure resource catalogue provides an extensive range of innovative Adventure accessories – from fleece balls to rubber chooks (chickens), floppy frisbees to boffers – to help you add to the fun in your program.

For a complete listing of books, games and gear, visit our website www.pa.org

TRAINING WORKSHOPS & SERVICES

Public training workshops are conducted throughout the USA, Australia, Japan and New Zealand which aim to help you learn the skills to present safe and valuable adventure-based programs.

Project Adventure also provides a wide range of services, including:

Challenge Ropes Course Design & Installation

Program Consultation

For a complete listing of workshop types and dates, visit our website www.pa.org

PROJECT ADVENTURE INTERNATIONAL NETWORK

Project Adventure, Inc.
701 Cabot Street
Beverly MA 01915 – 1027   USA

Phone (978) 524 4500 or (800) 468 8898
Fax (978) 524 4502   Web www.pa.org
Email info@pa.org

For more information on our licensed affiliates in Japan, New Zealand, Australia and Singapore, email international@pa.org or call (800) 468-8898.

Project Adventure has offices / partnerships in several southeast Asian, South American and European countries. Contact Project Adventure at (800) 468-8898 or info@pa.org for current contact details.

ABOUT THE AUTHOR

Mark Collard grew up in Melbourne Australia, the eldest of three children. He earned his Bachelor of Business (Accounting) degree, before heading to New York to study for his MBA – his eyes firmly set on the "tie and collar" world.

Then, having led programs with youth groups and summer camps in both Australia and the United States for many years, Mark's eyes were properly opened in 1989 when he attended his first Project Adventure workshop lead by Karl Rohnke. Things haven't been the same since.

Mark joined Project Adventure Australia in 1990, and was employed full-time by the organisation for ten years during which he was the principal manager, one of only two Certified Trainers in Australia, training coordina-tor, sometimes Challenge Course builder, and overall office dog's body.

Leaving PAA's full-time employ in 1999, Mark has continued to work free-lance for the Project, mostly worldwide, particularly in the United States and Southeast Asia. He chooses now to pursue his long-held dream to be an actor and voice professional, and is working toward his first Oscar!! You can check his progress at his web site www.mark-collard.com

Mark has been struck by lightning twice, can't back up a car towing a trailer to save himself, and has camped on the lawns of Australia's Parliament House for three days (as part of a logging protest). Mark lives in a mud-brick home in Melbourne's outer east, and counts his time with Project Adventure as some of the "funnest" times of his life.